ARCHITECTURAL PLANNING AND DESIGN OF BUILDINGS

Prof. Santosh Kinayekar

Dr. Prashant Bamane

Dr. Shobhan Kelkar

Dr. Akshay Wayal

Dr. Ajinkya Niphadkar

Prof. Amruta Raskar

Copyright

Dedication

This book is dedicated to all aspiring architects, designers, and planners who strive to shape the built environment with creativity, sustainability, and innovation.

To our mentors and educators, whose guidance and wisdom have inspired generations of professionals.

To our families and friends, whose unwavering support and encouragement have made this journey possible.

And to the visionaries who believe that architecture is more than just structures—it is an art, a science, and a responsibility to create spaces that enrich lives and stand the test of time.

With gratitude and humility,
Prof. Santosh Kinayekar

Dr. Prashant Bamane

Dr. Shobhan Kelkar

Dr. Akshay Wayal

Dr. Ajinkya Niphadkar

Prof. Amruta Raskar

Table of Contents

Acknowledgments

The journey of writing *Architectural Planning and Design of Buildings* has been an enriching and fulfilling experience, made possible through the guidance, support, and encouragement of many individuals.

First and foremost, I extend my deepest gratitude to my mentors and professors, whose invaluable teachings and insights have shaped my understanding of architecture and design. Their wisdom and encouragement have been instrumental in bringing this book to life.

I would like to sincerely thank my colleagues and peers in the field of architecture for their continuous support and thought-provoking discussions that have inspired many of the concepts explored in this book. Special appreciation goes to my students, whose curiosity and enthusiasm have been a constant source of motivation.

I am also grateful to my family and friends for their unwavering encouragement and patience throughout this journey. Their belief in my work has been a driving force in completing this book.

Lastly, I extend my appreciation to all those who have contributed directly or indirectly to this book—reviewers, editors, and publishers—whose valuable feedback and efforts have refined the content to make it a valuable resource for students, professionals, and architecture enthusiasts.

This book is dedicated to all aspiring architects and designers who strive to shape the built environment with creativity, functionality, and sustainability. May this book serve as a guiding light in your architectural journey.

Prof. Santosh Kinayekar

Dr. Prashant Bamane

Dr. Shobhan Kelkar

Dr. Akshay Wayal

Dr. Ajinkya Niphadkar

Prof. Amruta Raskar

Preface

Architecture is more than just designing structures; it is about creating spaces that enhance human experiences while ensuring functionality, sustainability, and aesthetics. *Architectural Planning and Design of Buildings* has been written to serve as a comprehensive guide for students, architects, and professionals seeking a deeper understanding of the fundamental principles and modern approaches in architectural planning and design.

This book covers essential aspects of architectural design, including site planning, space utilization, structural considerations, building services, and sustainability practices. It aims to provide a balanced blend of theoretical concepts and practical applications, enabling readers to approach architectural design with a holistic perspective. By integrating case studies, design principles, and contemporary challenges, this book encourages innovative thinking and problem-solving in architecture.

The motivation behind this book stems from the need to offer a structured and insightful resource that bridges the gap between academic learning and real-world architectural practice. With rapid advancements in technology, climate-responsive design, and urban planning, architects today must adapt to evolving demands. This book aims to equip readers with the knowledge and tools required to navigate these changes while upholding the principles of architectural excellence.

I hope this book serves as an inspiration and valuable reference for aspiring architects and professionals dedicated to shaping the built environment. Constructive feedback and insights from readers are always welcome, as they will help in refining future editions of this work.

Prof. Santosh Kinayekar

Dr. Prashant Bamane

Dr. Shobhan Kelkar

Dr. Akshay Wayal

Dr. Ajinkya Niphadkar

Prof. Amruta Raskar

CHAPTER - I

ARCHITECTURAL PRINCIPLES FOR PLANNING

Architectural planning and design of buildings is a process that involves conceptualizing, organizing and developing the structure with aesthetics of buildings to meet functional, social, cultural and environmental requirements. This process includes multiple phases, from understanding the client's needs to the final construction and post-construction evaluation.

1.1 Introduction

Historically, architecture was primarily focused on monumental and public buildings, reflecting the power, religion and cultural values of civilizations. However, over time the scope of architecture has broadened. Today, it covers everything from residential homes to urban infrastructure and its role has expanded to include sustainability, energy efficiency and social equity. The 21st century has brought about new challenges and opportunities for architects, with rapid urbanization, climate change and technological advancements. The practice of architecture is more dynamic than ever. Architects must navigate these changes while keeping the human experience at the core of their designs.

Architecture, often described as the art and science of designing spaces, transcends the mere creation of physical structures. It encompasses a profound understanding of how spaces shape human experiences and influence societies. In every corner of the built environment from towering skyscrapers to intimate residential homes. architectural planning and design play pivotal roles in defining the functionality, aesthetics and sustainability of the structure.

Architectural planning and design is a multidisciplinary process that merges creativity with technical expertise. It involves a thoughtful progression from conceptualizing ideas to constructing buildings that meet specific requirements. This process integrates various elements, such as the needs of the occupants, environmental impact, structural integrity, cultural context and regulatory constraints. Each phase, from the initial idea to post-construction evaluation is a critical thing in ensuring that the building is not only visually appealing but also functional, safe and sustainable.

One of the most significant in architectural design is the integration of technology in both design and construction processes. Computer-aided design (CAD) software, Building

Information Modeling (BIM) and parametric design tools allow architects to create more complex, efficient and sustainable buildings. Additionally, the construction industry has embraced advancements like prefabrication and modular building techniques, which reduce waste and speed up the construction process. Sustainability is now a key driver in architectural design. Architects are increasingly tasked with designing buildings that reduce energy consumption, use eco-friendly materials and minimize carbon footprints.

As architecture continues to evolve, its role in shaping cities, societies and lifestyles becomes even more significant. The buildings of the future will need to be flexible, adaptable and resilient to meet the ever-changing demands of urban populations. Architects will continue to push the boundaries of design, using new materials and technologies to create spaces that inspire, connect and protect.

This book aims to provide a comprehensive understanding of the architectural planning and design process, offering insights into the complexities of creating functional, sustainable and aesthetically engaging built environments. Whether you are an aspiring architect, a student or simply a curious reader, this journey through the world of architecture will offer a deep appreciation for the art and science of building design.

1.2 Principles of Architectural Planning

Planning is a process of pre thinking or pre arranging the things before an event take place or work take place. Architectural planning is a fundamental process that involves designing spaces that meet functional, aesthetic and social needs. The planning process requires a balance between creative design and practical considerations, including structural integrity, sustainability and compliance with regulations. Architectural planning is a complex process that requires a balance of creativity, functionality, sustainability and practicality. By adhering to these principles, architects and planners can design buildings that not only meet the needs of today's users but also adapt to future challenges for residential, public or commercial use. Good architectural planning enhances the quality of life, promotes environmental stewardship and creates lasting value for communities.

Purpose and Functionality:

The architectural planning of building must serve its intended purpose effectively. Whether the building is a home, office, school, hospital or public space, it must be designed to fulfill the needs of its users. The layout, circulation and organization of spaces should enhance the functionality of the building, making it easy to navigate and use.

User-Centric Design:

The needs, preferences and experiences of the end users should drive the design process. User-centric design focuses on creating environments that enhance the comfort, safety and well-being of the people who will occupy the building.

This approach often includes:

Incorporating human-scaled dimensions and ergonomics.

Ensuring accessibility for all, including people with disabilities.

Designing intuitive spaces that are easy to understand and navigate.

Sustainability and Environmental Responsibility:

Sustainable design principles aim to minimize the environmental impact of buildings. Energy-efficient systems, sustainable materials and eco-friendly construction practices are central to this principle. The goal is to reduce energy consumption, lower carbon emissions and create buildings that contribute positively to the environment.

This approach aspect includes:

Passive solar design to maximize natural lighting and ventilation.

Use of renewable energy sources like solar or wind.

Efficient use of water and energy.

Selection of environmental friendly materials.

Zoning and Spatial Organization:

Zoning refers to the division of a building into areas based on their use and function. Clear zoning creates a functional flow within the building, ensuring that different spaces are used efficiently and do not interfere with each other. For example, separating public areas from private or service areas it helps to maintain order and privacy in a building.

Important zoning considerations are:

Separation of quiet spaces (like bedrooms or libraries) from noisy areas (like living rooms or cafeterias).

Grouping related functions together (e.g. placing the kitchen near the dining room).

Creating logical paths for movement within the building.

Aesthetic Appeal and Visual Harmony:

While functionality is crucial, aesthetic appeal is equally important in architectural planning. A well-designed building creates a positive visual and emotional impact on its users. The building's form, materials and color scheme should work together to create a harmonious and pleasing environment.

The Aesthetic principles include:

Balance and proportion in the design.

Use of appropriate materials and finishes to reflect the character of the building.

Consideration of the building's context and surroundings, ensuring that it fits well within its environment.

Safety and Security:

Ensuring the safety and security of occupants is a fundamental principle of architectural planning. This includes designing for structural stability, fire safety and emergency evacuation as well as incorporating security measures to protect the building from potential threats.

The safety considerations include:

Compliance with local building codes and regulations.

Designing fire escape routes, exits and alarm systems.

Ensuring structural integrity against natural disasters like earthquakes, floods or storms.

Integrating security systems such as surveillance cameras, alarms and controlled access points.

Circulation and Flow:

The circulation of people and vehicles through the building is a critical aspect of architectural planning. Efficient circulation ensures that occupants can move through the building with ease, whether they are walking, using a wheelchair or driving.

The circulation principles include:

Designing clear, wide hallways and entrances.

Minimizing bottlenecks and dead ends.

Providing multiple routes for entering and exiting the building.

Incorporating vertical circulation elements like stairs, elevators and ramps.

Contextual Design and Site Considerations:

The building's location and surrounding environment play a significant role in its design. Contextual design considers factors like climate, topography and local culture to ensure the building fits harmoniously within its surroundings.

The site considerations include:

Maximizing views and natural light.

Orientation of the building to take advantage of prevailing winds and sunlight.

Respecting the natural landscape by minimizing environmental disruption.

Integrating the building into the community or urban fabric in a meaningful way.

Cost Efficiency and Budgeting:

Architectural planning must also consider cost efficiency and adhere to the project's budget. While it's essential to create innovative beautiful designs and the financial feasibility of the project cannot be overlooked.

The Cost Efficiency includes:

Value of engineering to balance cost, quality and performance.

Selection of durable materials that minimize maintenance costs.

Efficient use of space to avoid unnecessary construction expenses.

Planning for long-term sustainability to reduce operational costs.

Flexibility and Adaptability:

Buildings should be designed with future adaptability in mind. Over time, the needs of occupants and the functions of a building may change. Flexible planning ensures that spaces can be easily modified or repurposed without major structural changes.

Flexibility consideration includes:

Modular layouts that allow for reconfiguration of spaces.

Designing multi-purpose areas that can serve different functions as needed.

Planning for future technological advancements, such as incorporating smart building technologies.

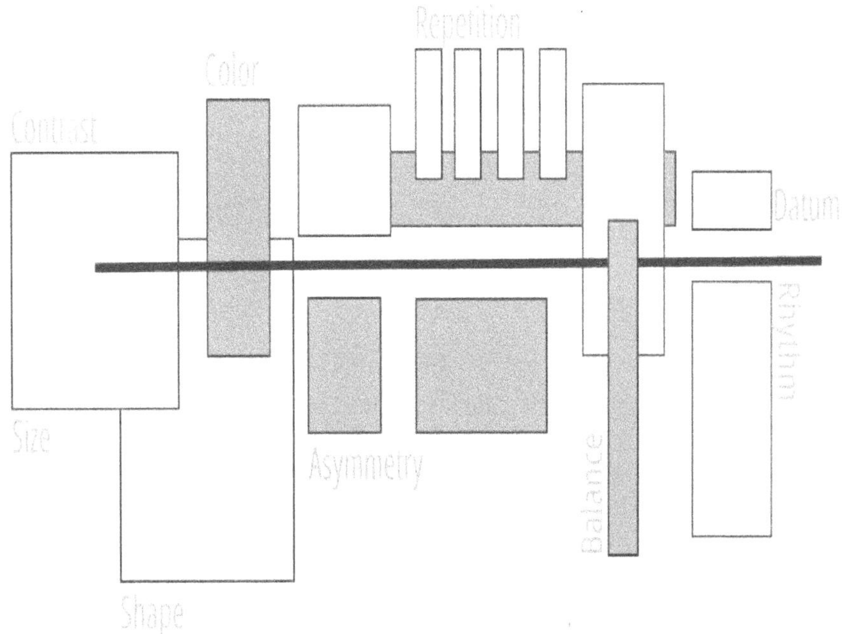

Fig. 1.1 Architectural Elements and Principles

Principles of Architectural Planning related to the Residential Building

The principles of residential planning revolve around creating homes that are functional, comfortable and aesthetically pleasing, while also being safe, sustainable and efficient. By focusing on aspects like zoning, privacy, ventilation, aesthetics and sustainability the architects and planners can design residential spaces that enhance the quality of life for occupants to meet their present and future needs. These guiding principles ensure that the residential design process produces not just a structure but a home that aligns with the lifestyle and aspirations of its inhabitants. Designing a residential building requires a deep understanding of how people live, interact and use spaces in their everyday lives. The objective is to create functional, comfortable and aesthetically pleasing homes that meet the needs of the inhabitants while adhering to practical considerations like safety, efficiency and sustainability.

Functionality and Space Utilization:

The importance of this principal is ensuring that the space serves the functional needs of the occupants. Residential buildings should be planned with efficiency in mind, allowing every square foot to contribute to the home's usability. Each area of the house, from the kitchen, bedrooms to the living areas and bathrooms, must be appropriately sized and positioned to serve its purpose.

Effective space utilization ensures:

A logical flow between different rooms (e.g. the kitchen close to the dining area and bedrooms located in quieter zones).

Properly sized rooms that accommodate furniture, circulation and storage.

Flexibility to adapt spaces for future changes (e.g. extra rooms that can serve as guest rooms, offices or play areas).

Orientation and Natural Light:

Proper orientation and access to natural light are critical in residential planning. Maximizing natural light improves energy efficiency, reduces the need of artificial lighting and enhances the occupants' well-being by creating bright with healthy living environments.

It includes:

Orienting living spaces like living rooms and bedrooms to the east or south to receive natural sunlight throughout the day.

Avoiding excessive exposure to the harsh afternoon sun, especially in hot climates by strategically placing windows or using shading devices.

Ensuring that kitchens, bathrooms and utility areas have good ventilation with lighting, even if located on the less sunny side.

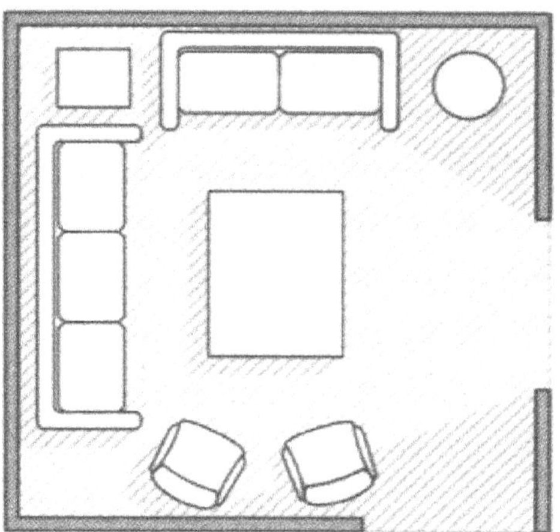

Fig. 1.2 Orientation and Natural Light

Privacy:

Privacy is a significant concern in residential buildings, both in terms of internal zoning and external considerations. Proper planning ensures that the layout offers privacy to the

13

occupants within their home and shields them from external disturbances, such as noise or views from neighboring properties.

Internal privacy: Bedrooms, bathrooms and personal spaces should be located away from high-traffic areas like the living room or kitchen to ensure quiet and seclusion.

External privacy: Windows, balconies and terraces should be positioned to avoid direct views into the home from neighboring properties or public streets. Fencing, landscaping and strategic window placement can enhance privacy.

Zoning of Spaces:

A well-planned residential building uses zoning to separate the home into different areas based on their function. Zoning ensures that the house operates efficiently and meets the occupants' lifestyle needs.

The typical zoning approach divides the home into:

Public Zone: This includes spaces like the living room, dining area and kitchen, where family members and visitors interact. These spaces should be easily accessible from the entrance.

Private Zone: Bedrooms, home offices and other private areas should be more secluded to ensure privacy and quiet.

Service Zone: Spaces like kitchens, bathrooms and laundry rooms fall under this category. Service areas should be easily accessible but designed to minimize disruption to the rest of the home.

Ventilation and Air Circulation:

Good air circulation is essential for comfort, health and energy efficiency. Residential buildings should be designed to allow for natural ventilation, reducing the need for artificial cooling and improving indoor air quality.

Effective ventilation can be achieved by:

Cross-ventilation by strategically placing windows on opposite walls to encourage airflow.

Well-ventilated kitchens and bathrooms to prevent the buildup of moisture, which can lead to mold growth.

Balconies, courtyards or terraces that allow air circulation while extending the living space.

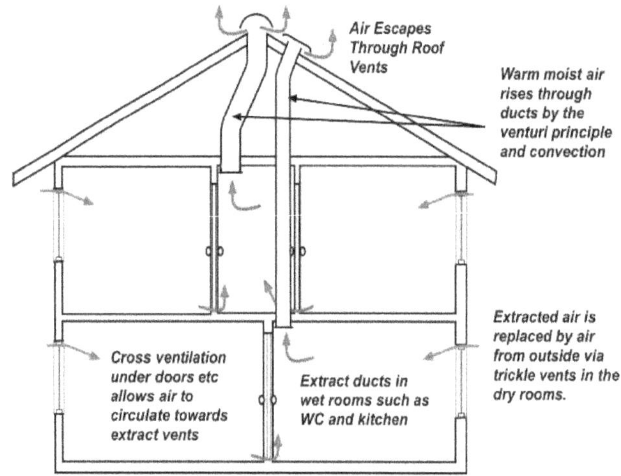

Fig. 1.3 Ventilation and Air Circulation

Safety and Security:

Safety is a non-negotiable aspect of residential building planning. The design should comply with local building codes and safety standards to protect inhabitants from potential hazards, both natural and man-made.

Safety measures includes:

Fire safety features like smoke detectors, fire alarms and escape routes.

Child safety features in family homes such as stair gates, window locks and non-slip flooring.

Secure entry points (doors, windows) and boundary protection (fences, gates, security systems) to safeguard against intruders.

Planning for natural disaster resilience, especially in areas prone to earthquakes, floods or hurricanes with appropriate structural reinforcements.

Comfort and Livability:

Residential planning should prioritize the comfort and livability of the home. Comfort is not only physical but also psychological, as the design of a home significantly influences how residents feel within it.

Comfort includes:

Room Proportions: Rooms should feel spacious without being overly large. High ceilings, well-sized windows and proportional furniture will help to achieve a balance of space and coziness.

Temperature Control: Proper insulation, shading devices and ventilation systems are critical for maintaining a comfortable indoor climate.

Acoustic Comfort: Good soundproofing between rooms and external noise sources ensures peace and quiet within the home.

Aesthetics and Design Harmony:

The word aesthetic indicates the physical appearance of the structure. While functionality is critical, the aesthetic appeal of a residential building cannot be overlooked. The design should reflect the tastes and preferences of the homeowners, contributing to their emotional connection with the space. A well-designed home balances form and function, creating an environment that is both beautiful and practical.

Elements that includes residential aesthetics are:

Proportion and Scale: Rooms, windows and doorways should be proportionate to the overall structure.

Material Selection: The choice of materials for walls, floors, ceilings and fixtures can greatly impact the aesthetic feel of the home. Natural materials like wood, stone or glass can create a warm with inviting atmosphere.

Color and Texture: Color schemes and textures should create a harmonious look throughout the house, enhancing visual appeal while maintaining a sense of cohesion.

Sustainability and Energy Efficiency:

Sustainable residential design not only reduces environmental impact but also enhances the long-term affordability and comfort of the home. Energy efficiency and sustainability are important considerations in modern residential planning.

Sustainable principles include:

Energy-Efficient Layout: Designing homes to take advantage of natural sunlight and ventilation which will ultimately reduce reliance on artificial heating, cooling and lighting.

Use of Renewable Resources: Solar panels, rainwater harvesting systems and green roofs are common features of eco-friendly homes.

Sustainable Materials: Incorporating eco-friendly, locally sourced and renewable materials can lower the building's environmental footprint and improve indoor air quality.

Cost and Budget Management: The planning process should account for the homeowner's budget to ensure that the building is economically viable without sacrificing essential quality.

Cost-effective planning includes:

Selecting materials and finishes that balance durability with affordability.

Designing compact and efficient layouts that minimize construction costs while maximizing usability.

Planning for future needs (such as additional rooms or spaces) to reduce costly renovations later.

Principles of Architectural Planning related to the Public Building

The architectural planning of public buildings requires a careful balance of functionality, accessibility, safety, sustainability and aesthetics. By adhering to these principles, architects and planners can create buildings that not only serve their intended purpose but also enhance the public experience, contribute positively to the urban environment and foster a sense of community. Public buildings are more than just physical structures, they are symbols of civic engagement, community values and public service. Public buildings serve a wide range of functions and cater to diverse groups of people. Whether it's a library, hospital, government office, school or community center, public buildings must be designed with particular attention to accessibility, efficiency, safety and the needs of the users. The architectural planning of these structures goes beyond aesthetics and functionality as it also plays a vital role in enhancing the public experience and the building's ability to serve its intended purpose.

Functionality and Purpose:

The design must prioritize the function, ensuring easy access to services, efficient space utilization, logical organization of rooms and facilities. Public buildings are designed to meet specific operational needs and every aspect of the layout should support these functions seamlessly.

For example:

A hospital requires carefully planned wards, operation theaters, emergency rooms and diagnostic areas that ensure smooth workflows for healthcare providers.

A library must balance quiet study areas with spaces for public interaction, digital resources and circulation of materials.

Accessibility and Inclusivity:

Public buildings must be accessible to all members of society, regardless of physical ability. Accessibility is a legal requirement in many jurisdictions and it is essential in promoting inclusivity and ensuring that everyone can use the building comfortably and independently.

Accessibility includes:

Barrier-free design: Wheelchair ramps, wide doorways, elevators and accessible restrooms.

Wayfinding: Clear signage and intuitive layouts that make navigation simple for people with disabilities or those unfamiliar with the building.

Universal design: Planning that goes beyond the minimum legal requirements to accommodate users of all ages and abilities, ensuring public spaces are welcoming to all.

Zoning and Spatial Organization:

Zoning involves dividing the building into distinct areas based on their use, ensuring efficient circulation and preventing overcrowding or confusion. Zoning also involves creating logical flows between spaces, ensuring that users can move between different areas of the building without confusion or unnecessary travel.

For example: in a school, classrooms should be zoned separately from administrative areas with recreational spaces located conveniently for students.

Public zones: Reception areas, lobbies and auditoriums that are open and easily accessible to the public.

Semi-public zones: Meeting rooms, offices or service desks where limited interaction occurs but privacy and security are necessary.

Private zones: Staff offices, storage rooms and other areas that are restricted from public access.

Safety and Security:

The safety of users is a paramount concern in public buildings. Architects must ensure that these buildings comply with safety codes, including fire safety, structural integrity and emergency evacuation procedures. Public buildings often house large numbers of people, so measures must be taken to ensure their safety in everyday use and during emergencies.

Safety features includes:

Fire safety: Emergency exits, fire alarms, fire-resistant materials and sprinkler systems.

Security systems: Surveillance cameras, secure entry points and access control in restricted areas.

Structural integrity: Planning for resilience against natural disasters (earthquakes, floods, storms), particularly in high-risk areas.

In addition, public buildings often incorporate systems to handle emergencies such as first-aid stations, panic alarms and adequate lighting for evacuation routes.

Flexibility and Adaptability:

Public buildings must be flexible enough to adapt to changing needs over time. The functions and requirements of public spaces often evolve due to societal changes, technological advancements or shifts in user behavior. Flexibility in design allows a public building to accommodate future needs without requiring significant reconstruction.

Modular designs that allow for reconfigurable spaces can accommodate different types of events or uses.

Multi-purpose spaces that can serve different functions depending on the need (e.g. a community hall that can function as a meeting space, event venue or lecture hall).

Easily upgradable infrastructure (e.g. adaptable wiring or plumbing) to integrate new technologies as they become available.

Flexibility ensures that the building remains relevant and functional throughout its lifespan, reducing the need for costly renovations or replacements.

Sustainability and Environmental Consideration:

Sustainability is an increasingly important principle in the planning of public buildings. Public structures have significant environmental footprints, so planning must focus on reducing energy consumption, minimizing waste and promoting eco-friendly construction practices.

Sustainable design principles include:

Energy efficiency: Using natural lighting, solar panels, efficient HVAC systems and insulation to reduce energy use.

Water conservation: Rainwater harvesting, water-efficient fixtures and greywater recycling systems.

Sustainable materials: Using recycled, locally sourced and renewable materials to reduce the environmental impact of construction.

Green spaces: Incorporating green roofs, urban gardens or courtyards to enhance biodiversity and improve air quality.

Public buildings should also aim for long-term sustainability, not just in their operation but throughout the building's lifecycle, from construction to eventual decommissioning.

Circulation and Movement:

Effective circulation within public buildings ensures that users can move through the space efficiently and intuitively. This principle is especially important in large or complex buildings like airports, hospitals or convention centers, where users need to navigate multiple areas without confusion.

Circulation involves:

Clear and wide corridors that allow for free movement without congestion.

Logical layout with direct routes to key facilities, minimizing the distance between high-use areas.

Wayfinding systems that include signage, color-coded paths and maps to guide visitors through the building.

In high-traffic public buildings, circulation planning also involves designing entrances, exits and lobbies to handle large crowds without causing bottlenecks.

Aesthetic Appeal and Public Image:

Public buildings are often representative of a community, government or organization and their aesthetic appeal plays a role in conveying that image. A well-designed public building should inspire pride, create a positive public perception and contribute to the overall urban fabric.

Aesthetic principle includes:

Architectural coherence: Ensuring the building's style and form align with its function and the surrounding environment. For example, a court house might employ a formal, monumental style, while a community center could use a more approachable and inviting design.

Material selection: Choosing materials that reflect the building's purpose, durability and maintenance requirements, while also contributing to its overall visual appeal.

Landscaping: Incorporating outdoor elements like parks, plazas or gardens that enhance the user experience and integrate the building into the larger context.

Aesthetics are not just about beauty, it is also an important aspect to create the atmosphere that can influence how people feel about using and interacting with the building.

Cost Efficiency and Budget Management:

While public buildings must meet high standards of functionality, safety and sustainability, they are often constrained by public budgets. Planning for cost efficiency involves making decisions that balance quality, durability and affordability without sacrificing the building's long-term usability.

Cost efficiency includes:

Value engineering: Identifying ways to reduce costs without compromising on essential features or quality.

Low-maintenance materials: Using durable, long-lasting materials that minimize ongoing maintenance costs.

Efficient layouts: Maximizing the use of available space to reduce the building's footprint and construction costs.

Public buildings should be designed for longevity and resilience, ensuring they can serve the community for decades without frequent repairs or renovations.

Community Engagement and Social Value:

Public buildings are often central to community life and their design should reflect the needs and aspirations of the people they serve. Engaging the community in the planning process can lead to designs that are more responsive to local needs and enhance the social value of the building.

Community engagement includes:

Inclusive design: Involving stakeholders and the community in the planning process ensures the building meets their expectations and addresses local concerns.

Public spaces: Creating open, flexible spaces where people can gather, socialize and engage in cultural or recreational activities.

Cultural sensitivity: Respecting local traditions, values and heritage in the building's design to foster a sense of ownership and pride among the community.

1.3 Codes of Practices

Codes of Practice for architectural and building design set the minimum standards for the safety, quality and sustainability of construction projects. These codes ensure that buildings are safe for occupants, comply with environmental guidelines and meet structural integrity requirements. These codes ensure that buildings are not only safe and habitable but also energy-efficient, sustainable and accessible. Compliance with these standards is often mandatory and regulated by local governments or international agencies.

Building Codes:

International Building Code (IBC): One of the most widely used model codes for building design, construction and safety. It covers various elements such as fire safety, structural integrity and accessibility.

National Building Codes (NBC): Each country usually has its own building codes. It covers all aspects of building planning, construction and safety.

Uniform Building Code (UBC): Used in some countries and provides a standardized approach to building safety, fire protection and structural design.

Fire Safety Codes:

NFPA (National Fire Protection Association) Codes: These codes are critical in ensuring fire safety in buildings. The NFPA 101 (Life Safety Code) is commonly used for building egress and fire protection.

Fire Resistance and Protection: Building materials and designs must comply with codes that ensure fire resistance for a specified duration.

Structural Codes:

Euro codes: These are European standards that provide a comprehensive framework for structural design.

American Concrete Institute (ACI) Codes: Focuses on concrete design and construction, including the ACI 318 for structural concrete.

American Institute of Steel Construction (AISC): Provides guidelines for steel structures.

ASCE 7 (Minimum Design Loads for Buildings and Other Structures): Establishes load considerations for structural design, including wind, seismic, snow and other environmental factors.

Accessibility Codes:

ADA Standards for Accessible Design (U.S.): These ensure that buildings are accessible to individuals with disabilities, focusing on aspects like ramps, doorways and restroom access.

Building Accessibility Standards (varies by region): Many countries have specific accessibility requirements, ensuring buildings are inclusive for all.

Environmental and Sustainability Standards:

LEED (Leadership in Energy and Environmental Design): A globally recognized green building certification system that promotes energy efficiency, water conservation and eco-friendly building materials.

BREEAM (Building Research Establishment Environmental Assessment Method): A British sustainability assessment method for infrastructure and buildings.

Green Building Codes: Many jurisdictions have adopted specific sustainability codes, such as the California Green Building Standards Code.

Electrical Codes:

National Electrical Code (NEC): A U.S. standard for safe electrical design, installation and inspection, widely followed for electrical safety.

International Electro Technical Commission (IEC) Standards: International standards related to electrical installations and equipment safety.

Plumbing Codes

Uniform Plumbing Code (UPC): A model code developed to govern the installation and inspection of plumbing systems to ensure their safety and functionality.

International Plumbing Code (IPC): Focuses on the installation, inspection and maintenance of plumbing systems worldwide.

Energy Codes:

ASHRAE Standards: Focus on energy efficiency, specifically the ASHRAE 90.1 standard, which deals with energy standards for buildings, except low-rise residential buildings.

International Energy Conservation Code (IECC): Provides minimum requirements for energy-efficient buildings.

Seismic and Wind Codes:

Seismic Codes: Standards such as the IBC, ASCE 7 and Euro code 8 provide guidelines for designing buildings to withstand seismic forces.

Wind Load Codes: Focuses on ensuring buildings can withstand wind forces, such as hurricanes or cyclones, based on local wind speed maps and codes like ASCE 7.

Safety and Occupational Health Codes:

Occupational Safety and Health Administration (OSHA): These regulations focus on ensuring a safe working environment during construction, addressing issues like scaffolding, fall protection and hazardous materials.

Personal Protective Equipment (PPE): Compliance with PPE guidelines to ensure worker safety on-site.

Urban Planning and Zoning Codes:

Zoning Codes: Local codes governing land use, building height, density and set-back requirements.

Master Plan Guidelines: Often provided by municipalities or urban authorities to guide the long-term development of urban areas.

Material Standards:

ISO Standards (International Organization for Standardization): Provides various standards for construction materials such as concrete, steel and wood.

ASTM International (American Society for Testing and Materials): Provides technical standards for materials, products, systems and services used in construction.

1.3.1 Code of Practice for Architectural and Building IS 962: 1989

The **IS 962: 1989** refers *to the Code of Practice for Architectural and Building Drawings in India. It provides guidelines and standardized practices for preparing architectural and building drawings used in the construction industry. It covers various aspects to ensure uniformity, clarity and accuracy in the preparation and presentation of architectural drawings. This standard helps to maintain a consistent practice in the field of architecture and ensures that drawings prepared by different professionals follow a uniform format, making them easily interpretable by all stakeholders in the construction process.*

Scope: The code specifies guidelines for the preparation of architectural and building drawings, ensuring that they are clear, easily readable and standardized.

Terminology: Defines common terms used in architectural and building drawings to avoid ambiguity.

Types of Drawings: The standard covers the various types of architectural and building drawings required for different stages of construction, such as Site plans, Floor plans, Elevations, Sections, Detail drawings, Structural layouts etc.

Scales: Specifies standard scales to be used for different types of drawings such as plans, elevations, sections, etc. Recommended scales are 1:100, 1:50 and 1:20. For different levels of detail in plans, sections and elevations, IS 962: 1989 defines the scale to be used in different types of drawings.

For example:

Site plans: 1:1000, 1:500, 1:200

Floor plans, sections and elevations: 1:150, 1:100, 1:50

Detail drawings: 1:20, 1:10, 1:5, 1:2

Lines and Symbols: Standardization of line thickness, types (dashed, solid) and other symbols to represent different construction elements like walls, doors, windows etc.

Dimensioning: Guidelines for dimensioning on drawings, including the placement, orientation and size of dimension text.

Projections: Specifies the use of orthographic projection for presenting views like floor plans, elevations and sections. The isometric projections for clarity in architectural representation.

Annotations and Titles: Standardizes the format for titles, legends and annotations used in the drawings for clarity.

Drawing Layout and Presentation: Includes guidelines on drawing sheet sizes (A0, A1, A2, A3 etc.), margins, title blocks and the organization of information on the sheet.

Site Plans and Key Plans: Guidelines for preparing site and key plans, indicating how to show plot boundaries, access roads and adjacent structures.

Building Sections and Elevations: Recommendations for how to present cross-sections and elevations, specifying the number of sections needed for clarity.

Lettering and Numbering: Specifies standard lettering heights and styles for labeling to ensure readability. Title blocks are also standardized, containing information such as project name, client, architect, scale, date and revision numbers.

Representation of Materials: Specifies how different building materials (brick, stone, concrete, wood etc.) should be represented in section and detail drawings.

Importance of IS 962:1989:

Uniformity: Ensures uniformity in architectural and construction drawings, making them easier to interpret and reducing the risk of miscommunication.

Efficiency: Standardized drawings improve the efficiency of both design and construction processes.

Compliance: Helps designers comply with regulatory requirements in the Indian construction industry.

1.3.2 International Building Code (IBC):

IBC is a model building code developed by the International Code Council (ICC) and is widely adopted throughout the United States and internationally. It provides a set of minimum standards for the design, construction and maintenance of buildings to ensure public safety, health and general welfare. The IBC addresses aspects like structural integrity, fire protection, life safety, accessibility and energy efficiency. The use of IBC is to create safe, sustainable and resilient buildings that meet modern construction standards and protect public health and welfare.

History and Purpose: The IBC was first published in 2000, consolidating several regional codes that existed previously such as the Uniform Building Code (UBC), Building Officials and Code Administrators (BOCA) and the Standard Building Code (SBC). The main purpose is to create uniform regulations that ensure buildings are safe and durable while streamlining the design and permitting process across different jurisdictions.

Organization: The IBC is organized into several sections that address different aspects of building safety and design, including

Administration: Defines how the code is to be applied, enforced and amended by local authorities.

Building Planning: Covers aspects such as use and occupancy classification, general building height, area limitations and types of construction.

Fire Protection: Provides standards for fire-resistive construction, fire protection systems and other fire safety measures.

Means of Egress: Deals with requirements for exits, including the number, location, dimensions and accessibility of exits from buildings.

Accessibility: Addresses design criteria for accessibility, ensuring that buildings are usable by individuals with disabilities.

Structural Provisions: Focuses on requirements for load-bearing walls, floors, roofs, including seismic, wind and snow loads.

Material Specifications: Includes guidelines for the use of building materials such as wood, steel, concrete and masonry.

Energy Efficiency: Works in conjunction with the International Energy Conservation Code (IECC) to improve the energy performance of buildings.

Seismic Design: The code includes seismic provisions based on geographic location, helping ensure that buildings are designed to resist earthquake forces.

Wind Load Provisions: Ensures that buildings are designed to withstand wind forces, including hurricanes and tornadoes, depending on regional risks.

Sustainability: While IBC primarily focuses on safety, it has provisions that encourage sustainable design and energy efficiency, aligned with the International Green Construction Code (IGCC).

Classifications of Buildings based on Use and Occupancy:

The IBC classifies buildings according to their use and occupancy, which influences the construction type, fire protection measures, allowable height and area.

Some of the common classifications includes:

Assembly (Group A): Buildings for gatherings of people (Theaters, Stadiums).

Business (Group B): Office buildings, clinics and other non-industrial workspaces.

Residential (Group R): Single-family homes, apartments, hotels and dormitories.

Institutional (Group I): Hospitals, jails and other facilities where occupants might need assistance during emergencies.

Educational (Group E): Schools, colleges and educational facilities.

Industrial (Group F): Factories and manufacturing facilities.

1.3.3 Local Regulations and Byelaws

Local Regulations and Byelaws are specific rules established by local governments or municipal authorities to regulate various activities within their jurisdiction. These regulations complement national laws and codes, addressing the unique needs, conditions and challenges of specific areas, cities or regions. In the context of building construction and development, byelaws provide more detailed rules than national building codes often shaped by local conditions such as geography, population density and environmental concerns.

Elements of Local Regulations and Byelaws:

Local Regulations: Rules established by local governing bodies (municipalities, city councils or local authorities) to manage land use, zoning, building development and public welfare.

Byelaws: Specific rules made by local authorities under powers conferred by legislation. They typically cover detailed provisions for building construction, land usage, sanitation and local infrastructure development.

Purpose: To ensure proper urban planning, manage infrastructure efficiently, address local environmental, safety concerns and enhance the quality of life in the community.

Areas Covered by Local Regulations and Byelaws:

Land Use and Zoning: Byelaws divide the city or town into zones (residential, commercial, industrial, mixed-use), regulating what kind of construction or development can occur in each zone.

Building Height and Density: Restrictions on the maximum height of buildings, floor-area ratio (FAR) and density of construction to ensure safety and prevent overcrowding.

Setback Requirements: Specifications about the minimum distance a building must maintain from roads, neighboring plots and other structures, ensuring proper space for ventilation, light and fire safety.

Roads and Access: Regulations for road widths, parking spaces, building access points for pedestrians and vehicles. Local authorities set standards to ease traffic flow and ensure public safety.

Environmental Regulations: Rules regarding tree plantations, rainwater harvesting, waste management and sewage systems, often influenced by local environmental conditions.

Architectural Control: In certain historic or culturally significant areas, byelaws may dictate specific architectural styles, color schemes and building materials to preserve the cultural heritage.

Safety Standards: Provisions for fire safety, emergency exits, lighting, ventilation and sanitation specific to local conditions.

Infrastructure Development: Provisions for water supply, drainage systems, electricity and communications infrastructure to ensure the city can manage the load from new developments.

Heritage Preservation: Regulations to protect historical buildings, landmarks and heritage sites. Any new construction near such sites may need special permissions to ensure preservation.

Components of Local Building Byelaws:

Zoning Regulations: Dividing a city into different zones and specifying what activities can take place in each zone (Residential, Commercial and Industrial).

Coverage and Floor Space Index (FSI): Regulations governing how much of the plot area can be built upon (coverage) and how much total floor space can be built (FSI or FAR).

Building Line and Setbacks: Guidelines to maintain space between buildings and roads or between neighboring properties. Ensuring proper light, ventilation and fire safety.

Height Restrictions: Rules limiting the height of buildings depending on the area and infrastructure available, such as access to fire services.

Road Widths and Parking: Specifying the minimum width of roads and the parking space requirements for different types of buildings (residential, commercial etc.).

Sanitation and Drainage: Local authorities set requirements for drainage systems, waste management, septic tanks and sewage treatment facilities.

Rainwater Harvesting and Green Buildings: In many places, local authorities encourage or mandate rainwater harvesting systems and energy-efficient building designs.

Lighting and Ventilation: Byelaws specify minimum standards for natural light and ventilation in residential and commercial buildings.

Implementation and Enforcement:

Municipal Authorities: Local regulations and byelaws are enforced by municipal corporations, city councils or local development authorities. For example, in a city like Delhi, the Municipal Corporation of Delhi (MCD) would oversee such regulations.

Building Plan Approval: Local authorities often require that building plans conform to byelaws and must be approved before construction begins.

Occupancy Certificates: Once construction is complete, a local authority inspects the building for compliance with the approved plan and issues an occupancy certificate, allowing the building to be used.

Considerations:

Legal Compliance: Builders and developers must ensure that their projects adhere to local byelaws, as non-compliance can lead to penalties, demolition orders or legal action.

Periodic Updates: Byelaws may change with time, especially in growing cities where infrastructure needs evolve. It is important to check for updates or amendments.

Local Adaptations: Byelaws may differ from one municipality to another within the same country due to differences in local environmental conditions, population density or socio-economic factors.

Sustainability and Environment: In recent years, many local authorities have been incorporating sustainability goals, such as mandatory solar panels, green spaces or energy-efficient building designs.

Example of Byelaws in Indian Cities:

Delhi Master Plan: The Master Plan for Delhi outlines zoning and land use policies, as it is supplemented by detailed building byelaws, which control construction and development.

Bangalore Building Byelaws: The Bangalore Development Authority (BDA) enforces rules for setbacks, FAR, road width and parking. Specific provisions are also made for the preservation of open spaces, green belts and water bodies.

Mumbai Development Control Regulations (DCR): These are comprehensive rules regulating land use, development permissions, FSI, setbacks and urban infrastructure to control the urban sprawl of Mumbai.

Challenges:

Compliance Issues: In some areas, there are challenges in ensuring builders and developers comply with local regulations, especially in fast-growing cities.

Coordination with National Codes: There may be discrepancies between national building codes and local byelaws, creating confusion for builders and planners.

Overcrowding and Urban Sprawl: Poor enforcement of byelaws in certain areas can lead to overcrowding, illegal constructions or poor-quality buildings.

Role of Citizens:

Public Participation: Local regulations and byelaws often include a provision for public consultation, where citizens can voice concerns regarding construction projects or urban planning decisions.

Monitoring and Reporting: Citizens play a role in ensuring that illegal or unsafe construction is reported to authorities, helping maintain the integrity of the urban environment.

1.3.4 National Building Code (NBC)

The National Building Code (NBC) is a comprehensive set of guidelines and regulations designed to ensure the safety, sustainability and efficiency of construction projects. These codes provide standards for design, materials, construction practices and safety measures that must be followed for buildings and other structures. Different countries have their own versions of National Building Codes, tailored to local climate, geography, building practices and risk factors like earthquakes, floods, fire etc.

Purpose of NBC:

Safety: Ensure the structural integrity of buildings to protect occupants and the general public.

Health: Maintain a healthy environment through proper sanitation, lighting and ventilation standards.

Fire Protection: Minimize risks of fire, establish fire-resistant design standards and ensure evacuation measures.

Environmental Protection: Encourage energy efficiency and sustainable building practices.

Accessibility: Promote inclusive designs that cater to people with disabilities.

Aesthetic and Functional Standards: Maintain structural aesthetics without compromising functionality.

Components of NBC:

Building Planning: Zoning regulations, architectural design standards, use of space and site development.

Structural Design: Standards for designing the framework of buildings, ensuring safety from natural calamities like earthquakes, cyclones etc.

Fire and Life Safety: Specifications on fire-resistant materials, fire detection systems, fire exits, emergency lighting and escape routes.

Building Services: Provisions related to plumbing, sanitation, electrical systems, heating, ventilation and air-conditioning.

Sustainability: Standards for energy-efficient systems, water conservation, waste management and use of eco-friendly materials.

Building Materials: Specifications for the quality and type of materials used for construction (cement, steel, wood etc.).

Accessibility Standards: Guidelines for ensuring that buildings are accessible to persons with disabilities, with ramps, tactile paths, elevators etc.

Construction Management and Practices: Guidance on execution of construction projects, quality control, project management and safety of construction workers.

1.3.5 Study of Sun Path Diagram, Wind Rose Diagram and Sun Shading Devices

Studying the sun path diagram, wind rose diagram and sun shading devices is essential for architects, urban planners and engineers when designing buildings and outdoor spaces that are energy-efficient, comfortable and environmentally friendly. These tools helps to optimize a natural resource like sunlight and wind while minimizing adverse effects such as overheating, glare or strong winds. When designing a building or outdoor space, the sun path diagram, wind rose diagram, and sun shading devices work together to create a climate responsive design. The sun path diagram informs window orientation and shading device placement. The wind rose diagram helps in harnessing natural ventilation by optimizing building orientation and positioning openings. Sun shading devices also helps to enhance thermal comfort by blocking excessive solar radiation, reducing energy consumption for cooling and providing a better indoor environment.

Sun Path Diagram:

A sun path diagram is a graphical representation of the sun's trajectory across the sky at a specific location over the course of a day and year. This diagram is crucial for understanding how the sun interacts with buildings, which helps in designing for natural lighting, energy efficiency and shading.

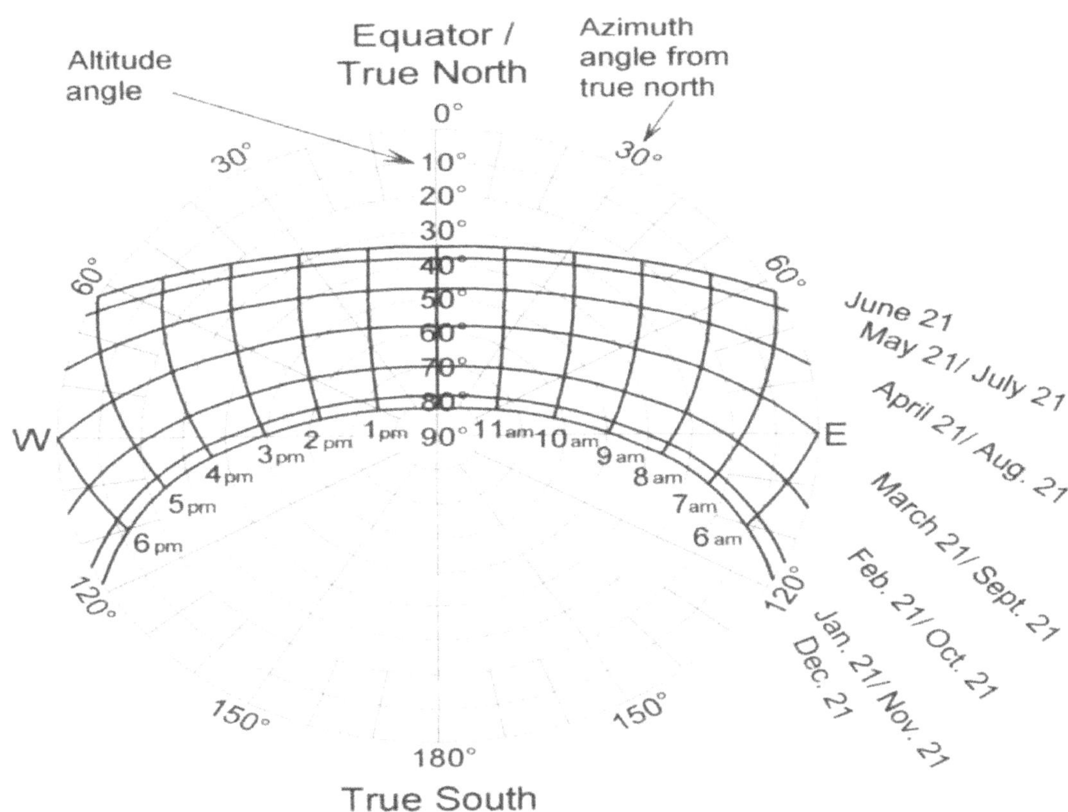

Fig. 1.4 Sun Path Diagram

Elements of Sun Path Diagram:

Solar Altitude: The angle of the sun above the horizon. This varies with time of day and season.

Solar Azimuth: The compass direction from which the sunlight is coming, measured in degrees (0° = North, 90° = East etc.).

Equinoxes and Solstices: The diagram typically shows the sun's path on key dates like spring and fall equinoxes (March 21 and September 21), also in the summer and winter solstices (June 21 and December 21).

Seasonal Variation: The sun's path varies with the season, rising higher in summer and lower in winter in the northern hemisphere.

Location-Specific: Sun path diagrams differ based on the latitude of the site, affecting solar angles and day length.

Importance in Design:

Daylighting: Helps in determining the best orientation of windows and openings to maximize natural daylight while avoiding glare.

Thermal Comfort: Understanding the sun's path helps in placing windows and walls to reduce heat gain in summer and increase heat gain in winter (passive solar design).

Shading Solutions: Identifies areas where shading devices like louvers, overhangs or trees are needed to block excessive sunlight.

Photovoltaic Panels: Helps in placing solar panels for optimal exposure to sunlight throughout the year.

For example, In the northern hemisphere, buildings are typically oriented with large windows facing south to maximize winter sunlight. Shading devices are added to prevent overheating in summer when the sun is higher.

Wind Rose Diagram:

A wind rose diagram is a graphical tool used to represent wind speed and direction data at a particular location over a specific period (for a month, season or year). It shows the frequency and intensity of wind blowing from various directions.

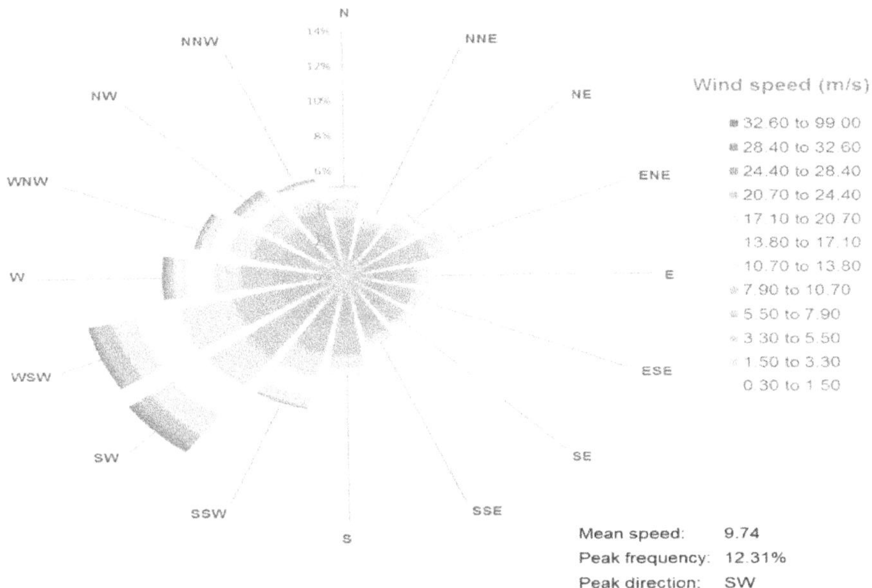

Fig. 1.5 Wind Rose Diagram

Elements of Wind Rose Diagram:

Direction: The diagram is a circular graph divided into 16 or 32 segments representing the compass directions (N, NE, E etc.).

Frequency: The length of each segment shows how often the wind blows from a particular direction.

Wind Speed: The segments are often color-coded to indicate different wind speeds (calm, moderate and strong winds).

Calm Conditions: The center of the diagram may indicate the percentage of time when there is little or no wind.

Importance in Design:

Ventilation and Air Circulation: Identifies the prevailing wind direction and helping in designing buildings that take advantage of natural ventilation with reducing the need of mechanical cooling.

Building Orientation: Helps in placing openings (like windows, doors or vents) to maximize cross-ventilation, especially in hot climates.

Wind Protection: In regions with strong winds, it helps in designing windbreaks (trees, walls) or orienting buildings to reduce wind impact.

Outdoor Comfort: Assists in planning outdoor spaces like courtyards, patios or walkways to be comfortable and sheltered from excessive wind.

For example, in a coastal area with strong prevailing winds from the west, the wind rose diagram would suggest orienting windows and ventilation systems toward the windward side for cooling, while using solid walls or vegetation to block wind on the leeward side.

Sun Shading Devices:

Sun shading devices are architectural elements designed to block or filter sunlight, reducing heat gain, glare and UV exposure. They can be fixed or movable, external or internal and are often customized based on the sun path at the location of the building.

Types of Sun Shading Devices:

Horizontal Louvers/Overhangs: Fixed or adjustable slats placed above windows, primarily used for south-facing windows (in the northern hemisphere). These block high-angle summer sun while allowing low-angle winter sun to enter.

Vertical Fins: Used for east- or west-facing windows, where the sun is lower in the sky. These vertical elements can block direct sunlight without reducing views.

Eggcrate Devices: A combination of horizontal and vertical elements, these offer protection from both high and low-angle sunlight, commonly used on east or west façades.

Brise-Soleil: A large architectural shading element (often a decorative screen or fixed slats) attached to the façade of a building to block sunlight.

External Awnings: Typically, fabric-based, retractable awnings can be installed to cover windows, patios or balconies to provide a flexible sun shading.

Green Roofs and Pergolas: Vegetation-based shading systems that use plants and vines to provide natural shading while improving the microclimate.

Interior Shades: Blinds, curtains or roller shades can block sunlight but they are less efficient than external shading because they don't stop heat from entering the building.

Importance **of Sun Shading Devices:**

Reducing Heat Gain: By blocking direct sunlight, shading devices lower indoor temperatures, reducing the need of air conditioning and saves energy.

Controlling Glare: Prevents harsh sunlight from causing glare on screens or reflective surfaces, enhancing comfort and productivity in office or living spaces.

Improving Aesthetics: Shading devices can add a dynamic aesthetic element to the building façade.

Energy Efficiency: Well-designed shading can reduce cooling loads in summer while allowing passive solar heating in winter.

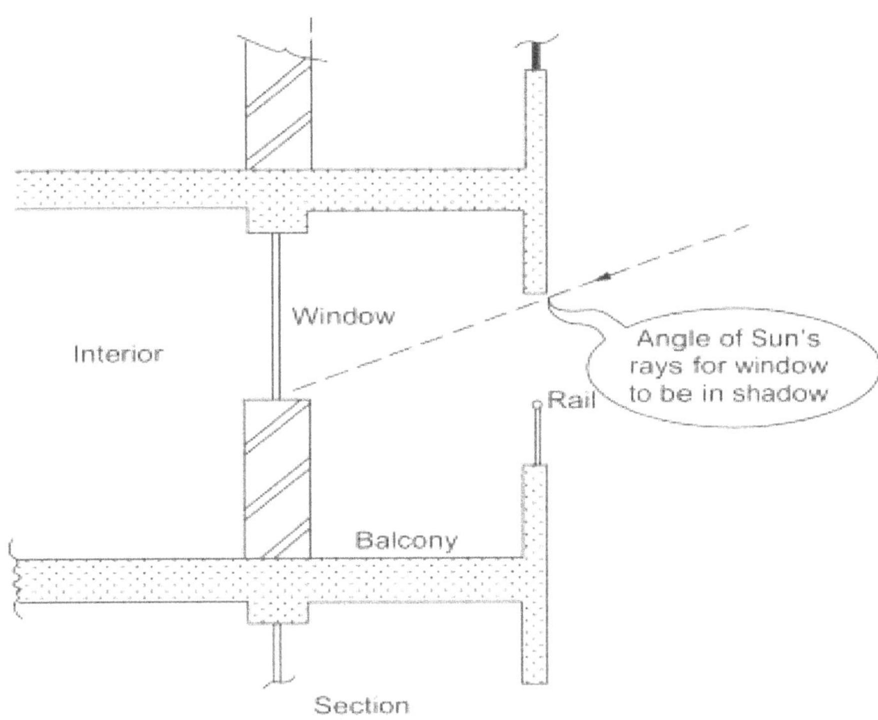

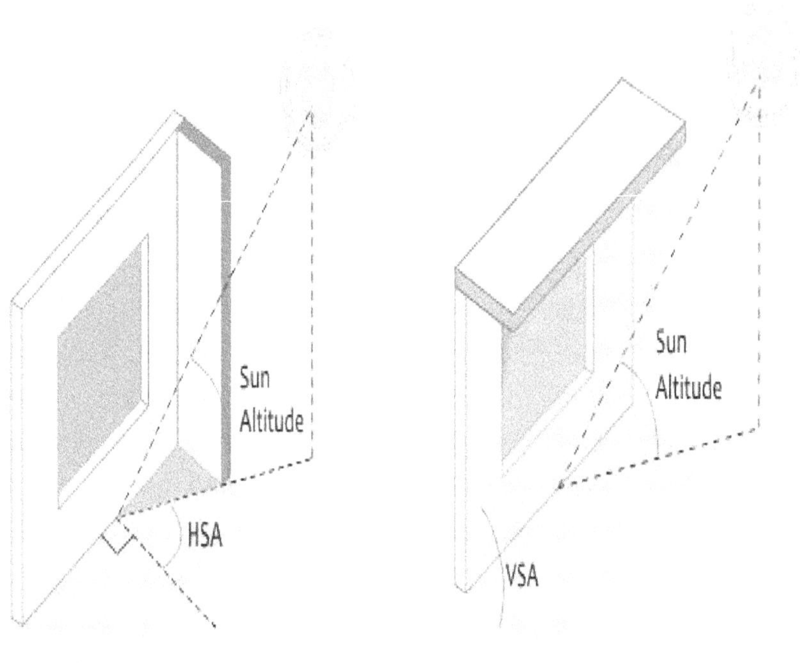

Fig. 1.6 Sun Shading Devices

1.3.6 Setback Distances, Carpet Area, Built-Up Area and Floor Space Index (FSI)

In the context of real estate, urban planning and building construction the terms like Setback Distances, Carpet Area, Built-Up Area and Floor Space Index (FSI) are used to define the size, placement and design of structures. These measurements are critical for complying with regulations, determining property values and optimizing space usage.

Setback Distances:

Setback refers to the minimum distance in a building or structure must be from property boundaries, roads or neighboring structures. This is mandated by local building byelaws or planning authorities. Setback distances are depending on local regulations, the type of road or street adjacent to the property, the building's purpose (residential, commercial, industrial) and the plot size.

Purpose: Setbacks ensure proper light, ventilation, privacy and safety (such as fire safety). They help to avoid overcrowding and maintain a harmonious urban layout.

Types of Setbacks:

Front Setback: Distance from the building to the front property line or street.

Side Setback: Distance from the building to the side property lines.

Rear Setback: Distance from the building to the rear property line.

Regulations: Local municipalities or development authorities, set minimum setback requirements in their building codes or zoning regulations. For example, in a residential area the local authorities might allow a minimum front setback of 3 meters from the street while side and rear setbacks might be 1.5 meters, depending on the plot size and building height.

Importance of Setback:

Privacy: Setbacks ensure that buildings are not too close to each other, maintaining privacy between adjacent properties.

Safety: Setbacks can provide space for firefighting and emergency access.

Aesthetics: Help in maintaining uniformity in the streetscape, contributing to the neighborhood's overall appearance.

Environmental: Setbacks can create space for greenery, landscaping or storm water management around the building.

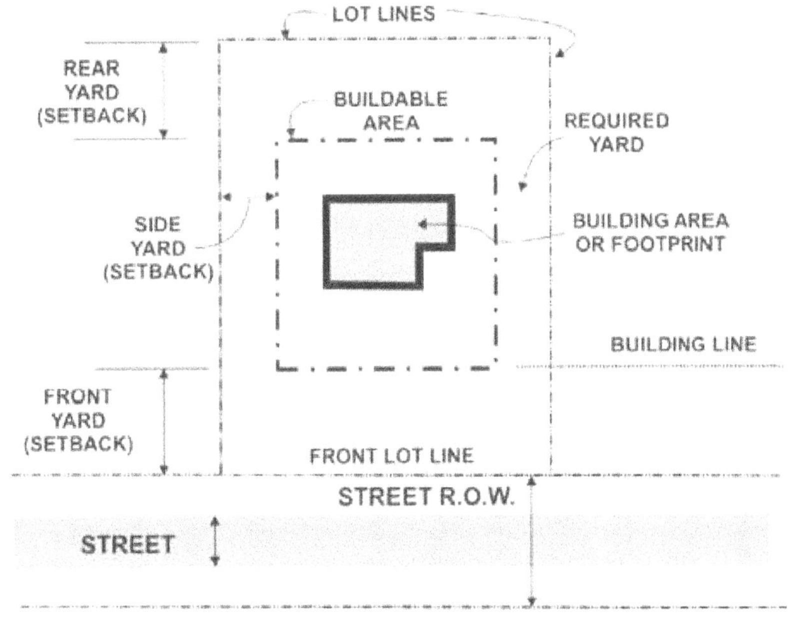

Fig. 1.7 Types of Setbacks

Carpet Area:

Carpet area is the actual usable area within the walls of a building or a specific unit in the building. It is the area where a carpet can be laid and is free from external and internal walls, balconies or utility areas. It is also defined as the net usable floor space inside a residential or commercial unit, excluding walls, columns, balconies, common areas (lobbies, staircases) and shafts.

Carpet area = Total area - Area of walls, shafts, balconies or common areas.

Importance of Carpet Area:

Since the carpet area represents the actual usable space available to the occupant, it is often the most significant metric for buyers and tenants. Carpet area allows potential buyers to make a better comparison between different properties based on usable space.

For example, in an apartment measuring 1,200 Sq. ft. of built-up area, the carpet area might be around 900 Sq. ft. It indicates the walls, balconies and utility spaces take up 300 Sq. ft.

Built-up Area:

Built-up area includes the carpet area plus the area occupied by walls and other fixed structural elements, such as balconies or terraces that may be part of the property.

Built-up area = Carpet area + Area of walls + Area of balcony/utility.

For example, if the carpet area of an apartment is 900 Sq. ft. and the walls occupy 150 Sq. ft. and the balcony 50 Sq. ft. then the built-up area would be 1,100 Sq. ft.

Importance of **Built-up Area**:

Built-up area gives a more comprehensive picture of the total space that is under ownership, though not all of it may be usable. Built-up area is often used by municipal bodies and authorities for calculating property taxes or construction permissions.

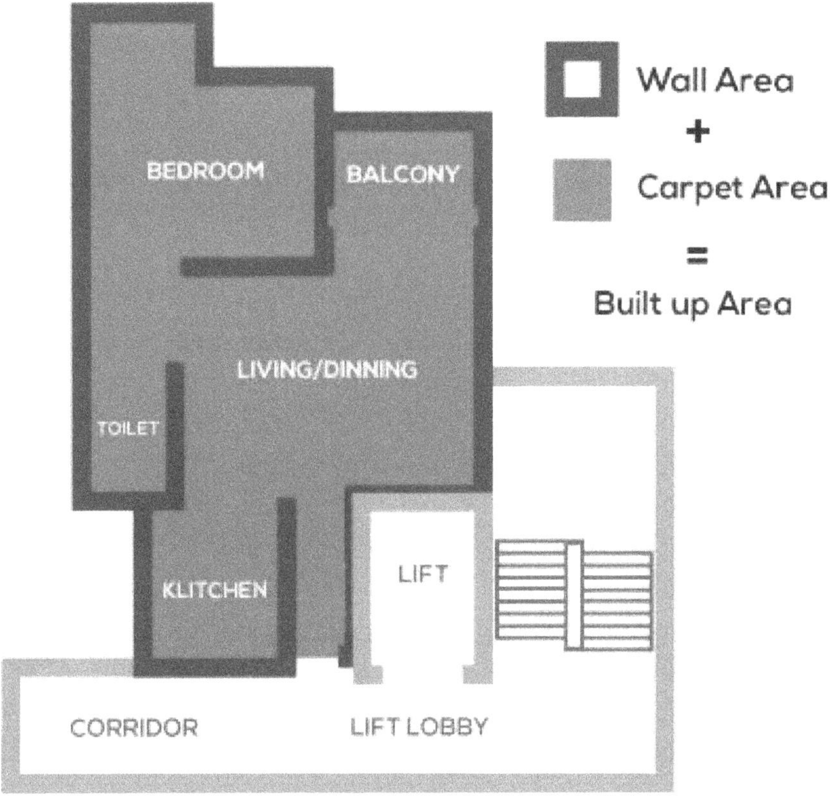

Fig. 1.8 Carpet Area and Built-up Area

Floor Space Index (FSI) or Floor Area Ratio (FAR):

Floor Space Index (FSI) is also known as Floor Area Ratio (FAR), is the ratio of a building's total built-up area to the total plot area it occupies. It indicates how much construction can be done on a particular plot of land and is governed by local urban development authorities.

FSI=Total Built-up Area of All Floors / Total Plot Area

Purpose of FSI:

FSI regulates the density of development, ensures adequate open spaces, sunlight and air circulation in urban areas. A higher FSI allows for more built-up area relative to the plot size.

Types of FSI:

Basic FSI: The maximum allowable FSI under standard conditions.

Premium FSI: In some places, developers can purchase additional FSI by paying a premium to the local authorities, allowing for taller or larger buildings.

Regulations:

FSI is regulated by local authorities based on zoning, infrastructure availability (roads, sewage, water supply) and urban planning goals. It varies between residential, commercial and industrial zones. Also it can be influenced by factors like the width of adjoining roads or proximity to public transportation.

Impact of FSI on Design:

FSI governs how many floors and how much floor area a building can have relative to the plot size. For example, an FSI of 2 on a 1,000 Sq. ft. plot means a total built-up area of 2,000 Sq. ft. can be constructed, which could be spread over multiple floors. (If a 1,000 Sq. ft. plot of land has an FSI of 2, the builder can construct a total of 2,000 Sq. ft. of built-up area. This could be 1,000 Sq. ft. on two floors or smaller units spread over more floors.)

Importance **of FSI**:

Control of Density: FSI helps control the density of an area by limiting how much construction can take place, ensuring urban areas remain livable and manageable.

Urban Planning: It balances the number of people with their activities in an area can support with the available infrastructure and amenities.

Real Estate Value: Higher FSI often translates to higher property values because it allows for more usable area on a given plot.

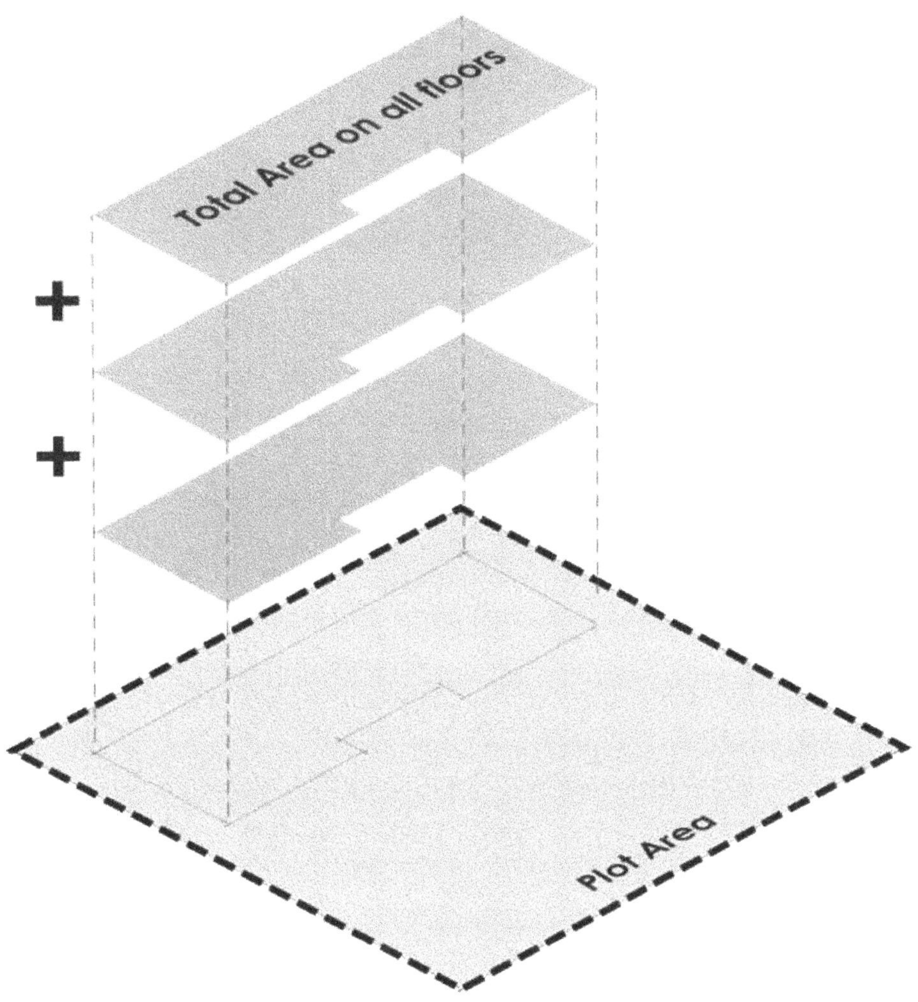

Fig. 1.9 Floor Space Index

CHAPTER – II

COMPONENTS AND BUILDING SERVICES

In the context of architecture, engineering and construction the components of building as well as building services are critical to create functional, safe and efficient structures. These components and services include all the essential systems with elements within a building that make it habitable, operational and sustainable. A building's components and services directly impact its functionality, longevity, safety and comfort. Careful design, material selection with integration of services are essential for creating buildings that meet regulatory standards, serve the intended purpose and contribute positively to the environment.

2.1 Components of Building

Building components are the foundational elements of construction. Each component serves a specific function, from structural support to interior aesthetics. It also plays a key role in the safety, durability and functionality of the building.

The Components of Building is mainly classified into 7 parts

1. Structural Framework

The structural framework is the backbone of a building which provides support and stability to the structure. It helps to withstand against loads, external forces like wind and seismic activity.

Foundations: The foundation anchors the building to the ground and distributes its load evenly. It includes shallow foundations (like strip or spread footings) and deep foundations (like piles).

Columns: Vertical elements that transfer loads from the roof, beams and upper floors down to the foundation. They are typically made of concrete, steel or wood.

Beams: Horizontal elements that bear loads between columns and it provides supports to floor. Beams also resist bending and distribute the load evenly to supports.

Walls: Load-bearing or non-load-bearing walls provide structural integrity and divide spaces. Exterior walls contribute to weather resistance and insulation.

2. Building Envelope

The building envelope is the exterior shell that separates the interior from the outdoors. It plays a major role in energy efficiency, weatherproofing and noise control.

Exterior Walls: These walls provide structural support and act as a barrier to weather, noise and pollution. Common materials include brick, concrete, wood and glass.

Roofing: The roof protects the building from environmental elements like rain, wind and sunlight. Roofs are often insulated to improve energy efficiency and can be flat or sloped depending on the climate and design.

Windows and Doors: These components allow light and ventilation into the building while keeping out rain, wind and noise. Energy-efficient glazing and well-insulated frames are used to minimize heat transfer.

Insulation: These are installed within walls, roofs and floors to reduce heat flow, making buildings more energy efficient and comfortable.

3. Interior Components

Interior components create functional and aesthetic indoor spaces. They include structural and non-structural elements that contribute to the building's appearance, acoustics, layouts etc.

Floors: Floors provide a durable walking surface and vary based on use of different materials such as concrete, wood, tiles or carpet. Floors may have finishes for specific aesthetic or functional needs.

Ceilings: Ceilings are the conceal structural elements which includes HVAC ducts and electrical wiring. They also influence the acoustics and lighting. Types include suspended, tray and dropped ceilings.

Partitions and Walls: Interior walls separate spaces and may be fixed or movable to allow flexible layouts. Materials include drywall, glass or timber.

Stairs, Ramps and Elevators: Essential for vertical circulation, these elements facilitate movement between floors and ensure accessibility for all occupants.

4. Mechanical Components

Mechanical components refer to systems that enable movement, improve functionality and provide comfort in the building.

HVAC Ducts and Ventilation Shafts: Ductwork distributes conditioned air throughout the building. Properly designed HVAC systems maintain indoor air quality and regulate temperature and humidity.

Plumbing Lines: Water supply and waste lines distribute clean water and remove wastewater. They include pipes, valves and fittings to deliver water efficiently.

Electrical and Data Cabling: Essential for power, lighting and communication systems. Cablings are typically hidden within walls, floors or ceilings.

5. Fire Protection Systems

Fire protection systems are essential for building safety and compliance with fire codes.

Fire-resistant Materials: Fire-resistant materials are used in structural elements to slow the spread of fire.

Smoke Detectors and Alarms: These sensors alert occupants to smoke or fire, giving time to evacuate.

Sprinkler Systems: Sprinklers automatically discharge water when a fire is detected. They are often installed in ceilings and activate in specific zones.

6. Sustainable Building Elements

Sustainability is increasingly central to building design with components chosen to minimize environmental impact and improve energy efficiency.

Green Roofs: These are planted rooftops that help manage storm water, reduce heat and provide insulation.

Solar Panels: Installed on roofs or walls and they generate renewable energy for the building.

Energy-Efficient Windows: Double or triple-glazed windows with low-emissivity coatings improve thermal performance and reduce heating.

7. Finishes and Aesthetics

The finishes and decorative elements of a building contribute to its aesthetic appeal and functionality.

Paints and Wall Coverings: These q2q`1enhance the appearance of walls and provide protection against wear and tear. Some coatings are chosen for durability, washability or acoustic properties.

Floor Finishes: Floor treatments like tiles, carpets and laminates add to the building's design while enhancing safety with comfort.

Fixtures and Fittings: This includes built-in cabinets, lighting fixtures and hardware which will add the utility to the spaces.

2.1.1 Staircase

Designing a staircase involves a mix of functional planning, safety considerations and aesthetic choices.

Basic Terms

Tread: Horizontal part of the step where the foot is placed.

Riser: Vertical part of the step that connects two treads.

Flight: Continuous series of steps between two landings or floors.

Landing: Platform between flights or at the top/bottom of a staircase.

Stringer: Inclined support running along each side of the stairs, holding up the treads and risers.

Balustrade: Guarding system that includes handrails, balusters and newel posts.

Headroom: Clear vertical space above each step, ensuring clearance as one ascends.

Preliminary Planning

Determine Location and Size: The location impacts space and shape (Straight, L-shaped, U-shaped, Spiral).

Building Codes and Regulations: Ensure compliance with local building codes.

Minimum tread depth: 10 to 11 inches (25 to 28 cm).

Maximum riser height: 7 to 8 inches (18 to 20 cm).

Minimum staircase width: 36 inches (91 cm).

Headroom Requirement: Minimum clearance from tread to ceiling.

Calculate Staircase Dimensions: Measure the total height from floor to floor and decide the number of steps based on riser height.

Types of Staircases

Straight: Simple and straightforward which is best for limited spaces.

L-Shaped: It includes a 90-degree turn which offers a landing for resting.

U-Shaped: It Makes a 180-degree turn and used in compact spaces.

Spiral: Circular in shape and improves esthetic appearance.

Curved: This type of staircase is a More elegant and have gradual curve. It requires a larger area and can be costly to build.

Design Considerations

Aesthetics and Material Selection

Wood: Popular for a warm and traditional look.

Metal: Durable and modern material which is sleek and space-efficient.

Glass: Contemporary and allows light flow which can be used for railings.

Concrete: Often used in modern or industrial work.

Ergonomics: Ensuring the stairs are easy and comfortable to climb. Avoid excessively steep risers or overly narrow treads.

Lighting: Use wall sconces, riser lighting or LED strips under treads for visibility and safety.

Safety and Accessibility

Handrails: It is essential for safety of the users.

Non-slip Treads: These are constructed by using non-slip materials or by applying non-slip strips.

Railing Height: Typically, 36 to 42 inches (91 to 107 cm) from the tread.

Visual Contrast: Add visual indicators for the edge of each tread to prevent tripping.

Accessibility: Consider ramps or elevators along the side of staircase for inclusive design.

Drawing Details

Plan View (Top View): Shows the layout and shape of the staircase within the floor plan.

Elevation View: Illustrates the side view of the stairs, showing the risers and treads in profile.

Section View: Provides a vertical cut through the staircase, showing headroom and structure.

Detail Drawings: For complex parts like handrails, balusters and newel posts the detailed drawings can be provided with precise dimensions.

Staircase Design Software

For the design of staircase even we can use the software like AutoCAD, SketchUp or Revit to create accurate and scaled drawings. These tools also allow 3D modeling, which helps to visualize the staircase in the intended space.

2.1.2 Foundations

Designing a foundation involves careful planning, structural calculations and detailed drawings to ensure stability as well as durability of the structure. Foundation distribute the vertical load over the subgrades at hard strata on the larger area of grounds.

Types of Foundations (Footings)

Shallow Foundations: The shallow foundation is applicable for lighter structure and relatively for stable soils.

Spread Footing: These are provided with individual square or rectangular in shape to support the columns.

Strip Footing: These are provided as Continuous footing under walls or rows of columns (combined footing).

Raft (Mat) Foundation: Large, single slab covering the entire building footprint, used when soil is weak.

Deep Foundations: Used for heavier structures or unstable soils.

Pile Foundation: Driven deep into the ground, reaching a stable soil layer.

Caisson Foundation: Similar to piles but larger in diameter, often drilled and cast on-site.

Factors Affecting Foundation Choice:

Type of soil

Load-bearing capacity of soil

Under ground water level

Seismic activity

Building load.

Foundation Planning

Soil Testing: Essential to understand the soil's bearing capacity, moisture content and composition.

Standard Tests: Soil boring, Standard Penetration Test (SPT) and soil analysis in labs.

Load Analysis: Calculate the loads (dead, live, wind, seismic) that the foundation must support.

Environmental Factors: Consider groundwater levels, seasonal variations, drainage and potential for soil erosion or frost heave in colder climates.

Code Compliance: Ensure compliance with local building codes and regulations, which outline minimum foundation depth, width and load-bearing requirements.

Budget Constraints: Budget requirement is related to different Factors such as cost of materials, labor, use of special equipment for excavation and soil stabilization.

Designing the Foundation

Determine Foundation Depth and Type: The foundation depth is based on soil test results, load analysis and environmental factors.

Structural Calculations:

Bearing Capacity: Ensure the soil can support the weight of the structure.

Settlement: Calculate immediate and long-term settlement to prevent uneven settling.

Shear and Moment Capacity: Ensure the foundation design resists bending and shearing under the loads.

Reinforcement Design:

Reinforced concrete is commonly used for foundations with steel rebar placed according to calculated loads and stresses. Design reinforcement for areas prone to high stress, especially near column connections and wall intersections.

Drainage and Waterproofing:

Install drainage pipes, gravel or geotextiles to prevent water buildup near foundations. Use waterproof membranes or coatings to protect foundations from water damage.

Foundation Drawing Details

Foundation Plan

It shows a top view of the foundation elements (footings, piles, mat foundation). Plan indicates dimensions, thickness, rebar placement and distances between elements.

Sectional Drawings

It includes section views through key areas such as under columns and walls. Section Shows soil layers, footing dimensions and rebar arrangements.

Detailing Reinforcement

Detailing provide detailed drawings for rebar layout, spacing and cover requirements (clear space between rebar and surface). Detailed drawing shows rebar positions in footings, along with overlaps and bentup details.

Elevation Views

Elevation shows the front view and side view. Also it shows the shape of foundation and depth of foundation with respect to ground level

Site Layout and Positioning

Level the uneven ground surface then starts marking the building layout on the site which includes boundaries, elevation lines and orientation. After fixing the boundaries mark all load-bearing elements like columns, walls and beams.

Foundation Design Software

The software like AutoCAD, Revit and SAP2000 are widely used for foundation design and modeling. Software offers accurate scaling, 3D visualization with structural analysis, making it easier to verify load and stress calculations.

2.1.3 Openings (Doors and Windows)

Planning and designing of openings is depends on various aspects such as functional, aesthetic and structural considerations.

Openings Overview

Purpose: Openings (doors, windows, vents) serve to provide access, natural light, ventilation, views and egress.

Placement: Strategic placement of openings affects light distribution, privacy, security and energy efficiency.

Structural Considerations: Openings should not compromise the structural integrity of walls. The lintels, headers or beams are often used above openings to carry loads safely.

Doors

Types of Doors:

Interior Doors: Used within the building to connect rooms.

Exterior Doors: Main entry doors and other exterior access doors, designed for security, insulation and weather resistance.

Specialty Doors:

Sliding Doors: Space-saving option, ideal for patios and rooms with limited swing space.

Folding Doors: Common in large openings, such as patios.

French Doors: Glass-paneled doors that swing open, often used for aesthetics and allowing light to pass between spaces.

Revolving/Automatic Doors: Typically used in commercial buildings for high-traffic areas.

Door Materials:

Wood: Traditional, customizable and versatile, but requires maintenance for weather resistance.

Metal: Steel or aluminum doors offer strength and durability; often used for security or industrial applications.

Glass: Common for sliding or French doors; tempered or laminated glass improves safety.

Fiberglass: This is much more useful as it offers visibility, durability and low maintenance also it is suitable for exterior doors with good insulation.

Composite Materials: It includes the combine wood fibers and resins for durability, strength and low maintenance.

Design Considerations:

Dimensions: Standard door heights are around 6'8" (203 cm), but this can vary.

Door Frames: Should be aligned with wall thickness, include weather stripping for exterior doors and often have adjustable hinges.

Insulation and Weatherproofing: Essential for exterior doors to reduce thermal transfer and prevent water penetration.

Security: For security purpose it is requiring to use Deadbolts, multi-point locking systems and reinforced frames for exterior doors.

Door Hardware:

Hinges: Hinges are provided for Standard swing doors and for heavy doors extra hinges are recommended.

Locks and Handles: They are varied based on function and security requirements.

Door Closers: Automatic closers are required for fire-rated doors and high-traffic commercial doors.

Thresholds and Weather Stripping: It prevent drafts, water and pests from entering.

Windows

Types of Windows:

`1   **Fixed Windows**: These are Non-openable window, mainly used for lights, views and modern designs.

Sliding Windows: Horizontal sliding windows are good for limited spaces.

Casement Windows: Hinged on one side, opening outward which will allow maximum ventilation.

Awning Windows: They are hinged at the top and provides ventilation while blocking rain. Often placed above or below fixed windows.

Double-Hung and Single-Hung Windows: Both have vertically sliding sashes but only one sash opens in single-hung windows.

Bay and Bow Windows: These are projected outward from the building to provide more interior space and larger views.

Skylights: Roof windows that bring in overhead light, often used in rooms with limited wall space.

Window Materials:

Wood: Naturally available and offers natural aesthetics but requires regular maintenance for weatherproofing.

Aluminum: Strong and lightweight, often used in commercial applications

Vinyl: Cost-effective, good insulation and low maintenance

Fiberglass: Durable and insulating which is suitable for various climates.

Composite: Combines wood and vinyl or aluminum which offers durability with minimum maintenance.

Single, Double or Triple Glazing: Multiple panes improve insulation and sound proofing.

Low-E Coatings: Reflect infrared light to reduce heat transfer which improves energy efficiency.

Tempered or Laminated Glass: It improves safety and security.

Tinted or Reflective Glass: Enhances privacy and reduces glare or solar gain.

Window Hardware:

Locks: Secure windows and prevent unauthorized access.

Latches and Cranks: Allow easy opening and closing for casement and awning windows.

Screens: These are added to operable windows to keep insects out while allowing airflow.

2.1.4 Roofs

Designing a roof involves selecting the appropriate type, materials, structural support and drainage system. Roofs are crucial for weather protection, insulation, aesthetics and structural integrity.

Types of Roofs

Flat Roof: These are provided with Minimal slope and commonly used in commercial buildings or modern residential architecture.

Gable Roof: Triangular shape with two sloping sides.

Hip Roof: All sides slope downwards to the walls.

Advantages: Stronger and more stable.

Disadvantages: More complex and costly construction.

Mansard Roof: Four-sided roof with two slopes on each side.

Shed Roof: Single sloping surface even called as mono-pitched roof.

Butterfly Roof: Two sections slope inward toward the center by resembling butterfly wings.

Advantages: Unique aesthetic and rainwater collection is potential.

Disadvantages: Requires effective drainage and complex waterproofing.

Gambrel Roof: Similar to a mansard but usually associated with barns and similar structures.

Advantages: Provides extra attic space, easy to frame.

Disadvantages: Not ideal for heavy snowfall areas.

Green Roof: Flat or slightly sloped roof covered with vegetation.

Advantages: Eco-friendly, insulates the building, manages storm water.

Disadvantages: Higher initial cost, requires structural support and maintenance.

2.2 Building services

Building services, often known as water supply, sanitary, Electrical and Plumbing services. These are essential systems that ensure the functionality, safety, comfort and efficiency of a building. They include heating, ventilation, air conditioning, lighting, water supply, drainage, fire protection and many more.

Heating, Ventilation and Air Conditioning (HVAC)

Heating includes Central heating systems (boilers, furnaces), radiant heating (underfloor, wall panels) and heat pumps. The fuel may be used as Natural gas, electricity, oil or renewable sources like geothermal. Ventilation require to removes stale air, controls humidity and ensures fresh air circulation. It includes natural ventilation (windows, vents), mechanical ventilation (fans, ducts) and hybrid systems. Air Conditioning includes different system such as Centralized systems (chillers, packaged rooftop units), split AC systems and ductless mini-splits. HVAC Controls the temperature and ventilation based on occupancy.

2.2.1 Water Supply

A building's water supply system is a critical component of its services, responsible for delivering potable water for drinking, washing, sanitation and other uses.

Components of Water Supply System

Water Source:

Municipal Supply: Water sourced from a public utility, usually treated and tested.

Groundwater (Well): Private wells provide water from aquifers but require pumps and filtration systems.

Rainwater Harvesting: Collects rainwater for non-potable uses

Pumping System:

Pumps: Used to maintain water pressure, especially for tall buildings where water needs to reach upper floors.

Types: Submersible pumps (for wells), booster pumps (for pressure management) and circulation pumps (for hot water).

Storage Tanks:

Stores water to maintain a constant supply during peak demand or in case of a supply interruption. Different types are overhead tanks, underground tanks and pressure tanks.

Pipe Network:

Distributes water from the source or storage tank to fixtures and appliances. Different pipes such as Copper (durable, corrosion-resistant), PVC (affordable, lightweight) and PEX (flexible, easy to install).

Valves and Controls:

Shut-Off Valves: Allows sections of the system to be isolated for maintenance or emergencies.

Pressure-Reducing Valves (PRVs): Controls water pressure to protect pipes and fixtures.

Backflow Prevention: Prevents contaminated water from flowing back into the supply and it is essential for potable water safety.

Fixtures and Outlets:

It includes taps, faucets, showers, toilets and water outlets for appliances.

2.2.2 Sanitary Layouts

Sanitary layout is a part of a building's plumbing system, focus on the efficient disposal of wastewater and sewage from fixtures like toilets, sinks and showers. These layouts help ensure sanitary waste is collected, directed safely to disposal points and prevents contamination of fresh water.

Components of Sanitary Layouts

Wastewater Collection Points:

Fixtures: Toilets, sinks, showers, bathtubs, urinals, floor drains and dishwashers all act as collection points for wastewater.

Traps: U-shaped pipes (P-traps or S-traps) installed below fixtures to hold water, preventing sewer gases from entering indoor spaces.

Drainage Pipes:

Collect and carry wastewater from fixtures to the main sewer line. PVC pipes are commonly used in residential and commercial buildings.

Branch Drains: Connect fixtures to main stacks or soil pipes.

Main Soil/Waste Stack: The main vertical pipe that carries all waste from branch drains down to the building's sewer line.

Vent Pipes:

Vents allow air to enter the drainage system, maintaining consistent pressure and enabling smooth wastewater flow.

Stack Vent: Runs vertically and connects directly to the main soil stack.

Vent Stack: A separate pipe that carries only air to prevent siphoning from traps.

Sewer Connection:

The point where all waste exits the building and connects to the municipal sewer line or an on-site treatment system like a septic tank.

Cleanouts:

Access points in pipes to remove blockages and allow maintenance. Typically placed at turns, long pipe runs or where the main sewer line exits the building.

Sewage Ejector Pump (if needed):

Used in buildings with basement bathrooms or fixtures below the main sewer line to Pump the sewage upward to the main sewer line.

2.2.3 Electrical Layouts

Electrical layouts are essential in planning the distribution of power, lighting and safety systems within a building. An electrical layout provides detailed schematics showing the positioning of electrical equipment, wiring and control systems to ensure the safety, efficiency, functionality etc.

Components of an Electrical Layout

Power Distribution Board (Main Panel and Sub Panel):

It receives electricity from the main source (utility or generator) and distributes it to various circuits. Typically includes circuit breakers, fuses and switches to control power flow and provide overload protection. Subpanel are the smaller distribution boards that serve specific sections of the building. It reduces the wiring length and improves load management.

Electrical Circuits:

Circuits distribute power to different parts of the building. They are usually categorized into lighting, power outlets and heavy appliances.

Lighting Circuits: Dedicated for lighting fixtures to ensure that lights remain operational even if other circuits trip.

Power Circuits: It serves as outlets and used for general-purposes in electrical equipment.

Dedicated Circuits: It is used in high-power devices such as Air conditioning, Refrigerators, ovens etc.

Wiring and Conduits:

Wiring carries electrical current between the power source and various devices. Copper or aluminum conductors are insulated to protect against electrical shock. Conduits are the enclosures that protect wires. These are made by PVC, metal or flexible materials. Conduits are often required in commercial buildings or where wires are exposed to physical impact.

Switches and Sockets:

Switches control the power flow to lights and appliances. They are available in various configurations like single-pole, three-way and dimmers. Sockets (Outlets) provide connection points for appliances and devices.

Lighting Fixtures:

It includes all types of lighting such as ceiling-mounted lights to wall sconces, task lighting and emergency lighting.

Emergency and Backup Power:

Systems such as generators used for uninterruptible power supplies (UPS) to maintain essential power during outages. Commonly used in hospitals, data centers and critical infrastructure.

Grounding System:

A system that safely diverts excess electricity to the earth to protect people and equipment from electrical faults. It includes grounding rods, wires and connections to all electrical components.

Types of Electrical Layout Plans

Lighting Layout: Layout plan shows the placement of all lighting fixtures, switches and associated wiring. Mainly used for, to balance light levels, to avoid shadows and to enhance functionality. It includes the details of fixture types, wattages and control systems.

Power Layout: This layout shows the location of all outlets, switches, appliances and dedicated circuits. These outlets help to manage power distribution and reduce overloads.

HVAC and Equipment Layout: This layout shows the power provisions for HVAC systems, kitchen appliances and large machinery. It includes the dedicated circuits, load requirements and specialized wiring.

Emergency Power Layout: Indicates circuits connected to backup systems (generators, UPS). It specifies critical circuits for lighting, elevators, fire alarms and essential equipment.

Communication and Data Layout: Shows placement of telephone, internet and other data connections. Often includes cable management and placement of network equipment for efficient data distribution.

Grounding Layout: This layout shows the grounding systems, locations and connections to ground rods.

CHAPTER – III

PERSPECTIVE DRAWINGS

Perspective drawings are an essential technique used in visual representation to depict three dimensional objects and spaces on a two-dimensional surface. This can be achieved by applying the principles of perspective, such as vanishing points, horizon lines and foreshortening. These drawings create the illusion of depth, proportion and realism. This technique is widely used by architects, interior designers, engineers and artists to illustrate how buildings, structures, interior spaces etc. would appear in the real world. Professionals can effectively convey their design concepts with aesthetic visions to clients, stakeholders and construction teams by employing perspective drawings. This technique enhances communication between professionals and clients, making it easier to understand design intent, spatial arrangements and visual aesthetics before actual construction or implementation. Perspective drawings is executed manually through traditional drawing methods using rulers, vanishing points and grids. Even it may be created digitally with advanced computer-aided design (CAD) software and 3D modeling programs. These drawings help in visualizing the final outcome of a project before construction or execution.

Elements of Perspective Drawing

Horizon Line: The horizon line is a level line that represents the viewer's eye level at where the sky meets the ground. In a perspective drawing the horizon line is crucial for determining the scale and placement of objects as it's the reference for vanishing points.

Vanishing Points: Points on the horizon line where parallel lines appear to converge. Vanishing points give depth to the drawing by guiding the viewer's eye into the distance.

Orthogonal Lines: The lines that recede toward vanishing points to define the depth of objects. They create a sense of distance and direction in a perspective drawing.

Station Point: The fixed position where the viewer or artist is observing the scene. It determines the angle and scope of the view which will helps to know the object position that how close or far objects appear.

Picture Plane: It is an imaginary plane placed between the viewer and the object being drawn. This plane represents the surface on which the drawing is projected.

Types of Perspective Drawings

One-Point Perspective: Has a single vanishing point on the horizon line. Often used to draw objects facing the viewer directly with all depth lines converging on the central vanishing point.

Two-Point Perspective: Features two vanishing points on the horizon line. Typically used to depict objects or buildings viewed from a corner, where both sides recede toward their respective vanishing points.

Three-Point Perspective: Uses three vanishing points, two on the horizon line and one above or below. It creates a sense of height or depth by adding a third vanishing point, ideal for viewing tall buildings or objects from an extreme angle.

Multi-Point Perspective: Involves more than three vanishing points, often used for complex or irregular shapes. Common in architectural and design presentations for dynamic or curvilinear forms.

Zero-Point Perspective: In this perspective drawing there is no use of vanishing point. They are commonly used to represent the natural landscapes or organic shapes where objects don't have straight lines converging to points.

Techniques for Creating Perspective Drawing

Establishing the Horizon Line and Vanishing Points: Start by determining the horizon line which is the viewer's eye level in the scene. Mark vanishing points along this line based on the type of perspective (one, two or three points).

Drawing Orthogonal and Transversal Lines:

Orthogonal Lines:

Extend from the object toward the vanishing points to create the impression of depth.

Transversal Lines:

Horizontal or vertical lines that establish the width and height of objects, crossing orthogonal to define shapes.

Foreshortening: A technique that compresses the appearance of objects as they recede into the distance, making them appear shorter than they are in reality. It helps to reinforce the perception of depth and distance.

Scaling Objects with Reference Lines: Use scaling techniques to adjust the size of objects proportionally as they recede. This can be done by dividing the ground plane into a grid, ensuring objects appear accurately sized at different depths.

Overlapping and Placement: Place closer objects in front of more distant ones to enhance depth perception. This technique of adjusting the scale for each object will helps to build spatial relationships within the drawing.

Light and Shadow: Adding shadows enhances realism and helps distinguish the placement and depth of objects. Determine the light source to accurately shade objects according to their distance and orientation.

Applications of Perspective Drawings

Architectural Visualizations:

Perspective drawings communicate the design intent for buildings, both interiors and exteriors. Used extensively in client presentations and design proposals.

Interior Design Layouts:

Perspective drawing shows furniture placement, room flow and lighting to help clients visualize finished spaces.

Urban Planning and Landscape Design:

Perspective drawings show spatial relationships in large-scale projects like neighborhoods, parks, and public spaces. Multi-point perspectives can provide an immersive view of complex layouts.

Product Design and Concept Art:

Perspective drawings are used in the early stages of product design to convey ideas about form and functionality. Also these drawings allow designers to explore and communicate ideas visually.

3.1 One-Point Perspective Drawing

A one-point perspective drawing is a method of creating the illusion of depth in a drawing using a single vanishing point on the horizon line. This technique is particularly useful for drawing subjects like roads, hallways, interiors or any scene where objects are viewed. A one-point perspective drawing is a highly effective technique for rendering the illusion of depth and spatial recession within a two-dimensional composition. This method utilizes a single vanishing point, strategically positioned along the horizon line in which all parallel lines converge as they extend into the distance. One-point perspective is particularly advantageous for depicting environments where the observer's viewpoint is perpendicular to the primary subject such as linear architectural spaces, expansive roadways, corridors, interiors and symmetrical structures.

Techniques for Creating One-Point Perspective Drawing

Establish the Horizon Line and Vanishing Point:

Draw a horizontal line across the drawing paper. This is the horizon line and represents the viewer's eye level. Choose a point on this line, typically near the center of the page as the vanishing point. All lines that recede into the distance will converge toward this single point.

Draw the Front Face of the Object:

Drawing begin with the front face (or closest side) of the object. This front face should be drawn without any perspective distortion.

Extend Orthogonal Lines to the Vanishing Point:

From each corner of the front face, draw orthogonal lines (also called convergence lines) that extend back to the vanishing point. These lines guide the depth of the object and will appear to shrink toward the vanishing point by creating the illusion of distance.

Draw the Back Face Using Transversal Lines:

Determine the depth of the object by drawing a transversal line (a horizontal line) between the orthogonal lines. This back face will appear smaller than the front face due to perspective, enhancing the illusion of depth.

Add Details and Additional Objects:

Draw other elements such as walls, windows or doors by repeating the same process. Drawing begin with a front facing shape then add orthogonal lines leading to the vanishing point. Keep all details consistent with the vanishing point to maintain perspective.

Shade and Add Texture:

Shading and textures can add realism to your drawing. Consider the light source and add shadows to highlights the objects wherever require.

3.2 Two-Point Perspective Drawing

Two-point perspective drawing is a technique used to create the illusion of depth and space on a flat surface by using two vanishing points located on the horizon line. This method is particularly effective for depicting objects or scenes viewed at an angle such as building corners or road intersections where lines recede toward two distinct points rather than one. Two-point perspective drawing is a powerful technique for conveying depth and spatial relationships in a scene. Mastering this method enhances your ability to create realistic and engaging illustrations. It is essential for architects, designers and artists.

Techniques for Creating Two-Point Perspective Drawing

Establish the Horizon Line and Vanishing Points:

Begin by drawing a horizontal line across your paper. This line is the horizon line and represents the viewer's eye level. Place two vanishing points on the horizon line, one on the left and one on the right. The distance between these points can vary based on how dramatic you want the perspective to appear.

Draw the Corner of the Object:

Start by drawing the corner of the object (a building) that faces the viewer. This can be a vertical line at the center of the drawing area. This vertical line represents the nearest edge of the object and will be the point from which all other lines extend.

Extend Orthogonal Lines to the Vanishing Points:

From the top and bottom ends of the vertical line, draw two orthogonal lines as one extending toward the left vanishing point and the other extending toward the right vanishing point. These lines will help to establish the width and depth of the object.

Create the Back Edges of the Object:

Decide how deep object is to be located and draw vertical lines from the ends of the orthogonal lines to create the back edges of the object. These vertical lines should be parallel to the initial vertical line.

Draw the Top Edge Using Transversal Lines:

Connect the tops of the back edges with a horizontal line to form the top face of the object. This line will create the illusion of depth as it stretches between the two orthogonal lines toward the vanishing points.

Add Details and Other Elements:

Draw additional features such as windows, doors or other architectural elements using the same principles. Use orthogonal lines that converge at the vanishing points to ensure they remain in perspective. Repeat the process for any additional objects in the scene, always referring back to the two vanishing points for consistency.

Shade and Add Texture:

Shading is required to give depth and dimension to the drawing.

CHAPTER – IV

TOWN PLANNING, ARCHITECTURAL TOWN PLANNING AND BUILT ENVIRONMENT

Town planning is the art and science of designing the urban spaces to create functional environments for people to live, work and interact. It is a multidisciplinary field that blends architecture, engineering, environmental science, sociology and economics to shape the built environment in a way that enhances quality of life. The concept of town planning dates back to ancient civilizations, where structured layouts were developed to ensure security, accessibility and resource management. The grid based cities like Indus Valley and Roman Empire are also design for the growth of towns and the modern smart cities of today, urban planning has continuously evolved to meet changing societal needs. In today's rapidly urbanizing world the effective town planning is more critical than ever. Cities and towns face challenges such as over population, traffic congestion, environmental degradation and inadequate infrastructure. Thoughtful planning can address these issues by promoting sustainable development, efficient land use, public transportation networks and green spaces.

4.1 Objectives of Town Planning

Town planning aims to create well organized, sustainable and livable urban environments that enhance the quality of life for residents.

Orderly Growth and Development

Town planning ensure the planned expansion of urban areas to prevent haphazard development. It locates different zones for efficient land use of residential, commercial, industrial and recreational zones.

Efficient Land Utilization

Planning allocate land for different purposes (housing, infrastructure, green spaces) in a balanced manner. Also it avoids overcrowding and ensure optimal use of available land.

Improved Transportation and Connectivity

The road networks and public transport systems are designed to reduce traffic congestion. Which will promote pedestrian friendly streets and cycling infrastructure for sustainable mobility.

Environmental Sustainability

Planning preserves the natural resources, green spaces and water bodies for the implementing eco-friendly policies, such as waste management and pollution control.

Adequate Infrastructure and Public Amenities

Ensuring proper water supply, sanitation, drainage and waste disposal. Public amenities such as healthcare, education, recreational facilities and emergency services.

Housing and Social Welfare

Promoting affordable housing to accommodate different income groups. Preventing slum formation and ensuring access to basic services.

Economic Development

Encouraging commercial, industrial and business growth. It creates employment opportunities by integrating economic hubs within urban plans.

Safety and Disaster Management

Planning for fire safety, flood control and earthquake resistant infrastructure. Implementing emergency response systems and resilient city planning.

Heritage and Aesthetic Considerations

Preserving historical and cultural landmarks within urban layouts. It also protects city aesthetics through architectural harmony and landscaping.

Smart and Future Ready Cities

Smart cities are Integrated with technology in governance, infrastructure and services for efficient city management. Also it encourages for the use of smart grids and automated traffic systems. A well planned town balances growth, sustainability and livability to ensure a better quality of life for current and future generations.

4.2 Architectural Town Planning

Architectural town planning is the process of designing and organizing urban spaces with a strong focus on aesthetics, functionality and sustainability. It integrates architectural principles with urban planning to create cities and towns that are not only efficient and practical but also visually appealing with culturally significant. This approach ensures a harmonious balance between infrastructure, green spaces, transportation systems and community areas while considering environmental impact, historical preservation, modern development needs etc.

Architectural town planning is a vital discipline that merges design excellence with urban functionality. It aims to create cities that are sustainable, resilient and visually inspiring while meeting the needs of growing populations. By integrating modern technology architects can shape vibrant, livable cities for future generations.

Architectural Town Planning includes following design points:

Zoning and Land Use Planning.

Urban Design and Aesthetic Considerations.

Infrastructure and Transportation Networks.

Sustainable and Eco-Friendly Design.

Smart City Planning.

Housing and Community Development.

Preservation of Heritage and Culture.

Environmental and Disaster Resilience.

Role of Architects in Town Planning:

a. Designing sustainable and aesthetically pleasing buildings.

b. Collaborating with urban planners, engineers and policymakers.

c. Ensuring functional and people-centric urban layouts.

d. Innovating smart and future ready architectural solutions.

Case Studies of Well Planned Cities:

Well planned cities around the world showcase the successful integration of architectural town planning principles. These cities prioritize sustainability, infrastructure, aesthetics and livability.

For Example,

1. **Chandigarh, India** – A Masterpiece of Modern Planning

2. **Brasília, Brazil** – A City Designed Like an Airplane

3. **Singapore – The Smart City Model**

4. **Copenhagen, Denmark – The Bicycle Friendly City**

5. **Amsterdam, Netherlands – A Water Centric Urban Plan**

4.2.1 Master Plan in Town Planning

A **master plan** is a long-term blueprint for urban development that outlines land use, infrastructure, housing, transportation, environmental management and economic growth strategies. It serves as a guide for policymakers, urban planners and developers to ensure **efficient** urban expansion. A well-structured master plan prevents haphazard development, ensures balanced resource distribution and improves the overall quality of life for residents.

Types of Master Plans:

a. Comprehensive Master Plan

b. Sectoral Master Plan

c. Regional Master Plan

d. Smart City Master Plan

Challenges in Implementing a Master Plan:

Land acquisition and resistance from communities.

Financial constraints and budget limitations.

Rapid population growth leading to unplanned urban expansion.

Environmental concerns and climate change impacts.

Coordination between multiple government agencies and stakeholders.

4.2.2 Re-Development of Buildings

Building re-development is the process of demolishing and reconstructing old, deteriorated or underutilized structures to improve urban infrastructure, maximize land use and enhance the quality of living. It plays an important role in **revitalizing cities**, ensuring **structural safety** and promoting **sustainable urban development**. With rapid urbanization, many cities face issues like **congestion and lack of modern amenities**. Re-development helps to tackle these challenges by introducing **modern housing, better facilities and improved urban aesthetics** while ensuring efficient land utilization.

Types of Building for Re-Development:

a. Residential Re-Development

b. Commercial Re-Development

c. Industrial Re-Development

d. Heritage Re-Development

Objectives of Re-Development:

Structural Safety & Upgradation

Better Land Utilization

Improved Infrastructure & Amenities

Urban Renewal & Aesthetic Enhancement

Environmental Sustainability

Affordable Housing & Social Benefits

Challenges in Re-Development:

Legal & Regulatory Issues

Financial Constraints

Resistance from Residents & Stakeholders

Environmental Impact

4.2.3 Slum Rehabilitation

Slum rehabilitation is the process of improving the living conditions of people residing in slums by providing better housing, infrastructure and amenities. The goal is to replace unhygienic, overcrowded and unsafe settlements with planned, sustainable and livable housing solutions while ensuring the socio-economy of slum dwellers. With rapid urbanization, slums have become a major challenge in many cities worldwide, leading to issues such as poor sanitation, lack of clean water, inadequate housing and unemployment. Proper rehabilitation programs help in integrating slum residents into the urban fabric while improving their quality of life.

Objectives of Slum Rehabilitation:

Types of Slum Rehabilitation Approaches:

1. In-Situ Rehabilitation (On-Site Redevelopment)

Slum dwellers are rehabilitated at the same location after reconstructing their homes. It prevents forced displacement and maintains social and economic ties.

Example: Mumbai's Dharavi Slum Redevelopment Project (India).

2. Relocation & Resettlement

Slum dwellers are moved to new housing projects on the city outskirts. It is followed in cases where slums are located in hazard-prone or environmentally sensitive areas.

3. Public Private Partnership (PPP) Models

Governments partner with private developers to build affordable housing for slum residents. Developers construct free housing for slum dwellers in exchange for the right to build commercial properties on surplus land.

Example: Slum Rehabilitation Authority (SRA) scheme in Mumbai, India.

4. Upgradation of Existing Slums

Instead of relocating slum dwellers, the focus is on improving existing infrastructure. It includes paving roads, installing water, sanitation facilities and strengthening housing structures.

Challenges in Slum Rehabilitation:

Land Ownership and Legal Issues

Resistance from Slum Dwellers

Financial Constraints

Poor Implementation and Corruption

Socio-Economic Barriers

4.3 Architectural Town Planning (Refer Chapter-I for more details)

4.3.1 Introduction

Architectural planning is the process of designing and organizing spaces to create functional, aesthetic and sustainable built environments. It involves the strategic arrangement of structures, spaces and utilities to optimize efficiency, comfort and safety while considering factors like climate, topography, urban context and user requirements.

A well-planned architectural design not only enhances the visual appeal of a structure but also ensures its structural integrity, energy efficiency and adaptability. The process integrates engineering principles, artistic creativity, environmental sustainability and user-centered design to produce buildings that are both practical and inspiring.

Objectives of Architectural Planning:

Functionality & Space Utilization

Aesthetic Appeal

Structural Stability & Safety

Environmental Sustainability

Economic Feasibility

Adaptability & Future Growth

4.3.2 Principles

Principles of Architectural Planning:

1. Unity & Harmony

2. Proportion & Scale

3. Balance & Symmetry

4. Light & Ventilation

5. Circulation & Accessibility

6. Sustainability & Eco-Friendliness

Types of Architectural Planning:

1. Residential Planning

Design of individual houses, apartments and gated communities.

2. Commercial & Office Planning

Includes shopping malls, corporate offices and business hubs.

3. Institutional & Public Buildings

Includes schools, hospitals, government offices and museums.

4. Industrial Planning

Focuses on factories, warehouses and manufacturing units.

5. Urban & Town Planning

Covers the design of entire cities, smart cities and sustainable townships.

Challenges in Architectural Planning:

Rapid urbanization leading to space constraints and infrastructure overload.

Budget limitations affecting design quality and sustainability.

Climatic challenges requiring adaptive architectural solutions.

Balancing tradition with modern innovation in cultural heritage areas.

Legal and regulatory approvals delaying project execution.

4.4 Built Environment

4.4.1 Introduction

The built environment refers to the man-made surroundings that provide the setting for human activities, ranging from buildings, infrastructure, public spaces and urban landscapes. It includes homes, schools, workplaces, parks, roads and utilities, all designed to meet human needs and support daily life. A well planned built environment plays a crucial role in economic growth, social well-being and environmental sustainability. It affects how people live, work and interact with their surroundings.

Components of the Built Environment:

1. Buildings & Structures

Residential Buildings (houses, apartments, townships)

Commercial Buildings (offices, shopping malls, hotels)

Industrial Buildings (factories, warehouses, power plants)

Institutional Buildings (schools, hospitals, government offices)

2. Infrastructure

Transport Networks (roads, railways, airports, bridges)

Utility Systems (water supply, sewage, electricity, telecommunications)

Energy Infrastructure (power plants, solar farms, wind turbines)

3. Public Spaces & Green Areas

Parks and Recreational Areas (gardens, playgrounds, waterfronts)

Community Spaces (plazas, markets, cultural centers)

Urban Landscaping (tree lined streets, pedestrian zones, cycling tracks)

4. Smart & Sustainable Features

Smart Cities (Automated traffic control)

Green Buildings (solar panels, rainwater harvesting, energy efficient design)

Waste Management Systems (recycling plants, sustainable disposal methods)

Importance of the Built Environment:

1. Enhances Quality of Life

Provides safe, comfortable and efficient living spaces.

Improves health and well-being with access to clean air, water and green spaces.

2. Supports Economic Growth

Attracts business investments, job creation and tourism.

Enhances real estate value and commercial opportunities.

3. Facilitates Connectivity & Mobility

Efficient transport networks reduce travel time and pollution.

Walkable cities promote sustainable urban mobility.

4. Ensures Environmental Sustainability

Reduces carbon footprint through green architecture and smart energy use.

Protects natural resources with eco-friendly infrastructure.

5. Promotes Social Interaction & Community Development

Well planned public spaces encourage community engagement.

Mixed use developments integrate residential, commercial and cultural spaces.

4.4.2 Principles of a Well-Planned Built Environment

The principles of the built environment ensure that human settlements are functional, sustainable, resilient and inclusive. By integrating environmental responsibility with smart technology, the cities and buildings can improve quality of life while minimizing their ecological footprint.

1. Functionality & Efficiency

Space should be optimized for practical use.

Urban planning should reduce congestion and promote accessibility.

2. Sustainability & Resilience

Integrate eco-friendly materials and energy efficient designs.

Ensure structures are resistant to natural disasters (Earthquakes, Floods).

3. Aesthetic & Cultural Integration

Preserve architectural heritage while embracing modern innovation.

Maintain visual harmony between buildings, streets and public areas.

4. Safety & Security

Include disaster preparedness features in city planning.

Implement well-lit streets, CCTV surveillance and emergency response systems.

5. Inclusivity & Accessibility

Ensure spaces are accessible for people with disabilities.

Provide affordable housing and community facilities.

Challenges in the Built Environment:

Rapid Urbanization: Unplanned growth leads to slums, overcrowding and pollution.

Infrastructure Deficits: Many cities lack adequate transport, sanitation and utilities.

Environmental Degradation: Poor planning contributes to deforestation, water pollution and climate change.

Affordability Issues: Rising land and construction costs limit housing for low income groups.

Examples of Well-Planned Built Environments Cities:

1. Singapore

2. Copenhagen, Denmark

3. Curitiba, Brazil

CHAPTER – V

GREEN BUILDINGS

A Green Building is a structure that is designed, constructed and operated in an environmentally responsible manner throughout its life cycle, from planning and design to construction, operation, maintenance, renovation and demolition. Green buildings reduce the environmental impact and promote sustainability by focusing on energy efficiency, water conservation, sustainable materials and smart technologies. They create a healthier and more resilient built environment. Green building materials are sustainable, energy-efficient and environmentally friendly. By using recycled, natural and low-carbon materials, buildings can reduce energy consumption, enhance durability and improve human well-being.

5.1 Introduction

Green buildings are a crucial step toward sustainable urban development, reducing energy use, water consumption and environmental impact. By adopting eco-friendly technologies with green certifications, the cities can enhance livability and promote a sustainable future. A Green Building is a structure that is designed, constructed and operated in an environmentally responsible and resource efficient manner throughout its life cycle. The goal of green buildings is to reduce negative environmental impacts, enhance energy efficiency, promote healthier living spaces and ensure sustainability for future generations. Green buildings focus on reducing waste, optimizing energy use, improving air and water quality with sustainable materials.

Benefits (Advantages) of Green Buildings:

1. Environmental Benefits

Reduces carbon footprint by minimizing energy consumption.

Prevents deforestation through sustainable material use.

Minimizes water wastage and encourages water conservation.

2. Economic Benefits

Lower energy and water bills due to efficiency measures.

Increased property value and market demand for eco-friendly buildings.

Government incentives and tax benefits for green certified buildings.

3. Health & Social Benefits

Improved indoor air quality reduces respiratory diseases and allergies.

It provides better natural lighting.

Green Building Rating Systems & Certifications:

1. LEED (Leadership in Energy and Environmental Design)

2. BREEAM (Building Research Establishment Environmental Assessment Method)

3. IGBC (Indian Green Building Council)

4. GRIHA (Green Rating for Integrated Habitat Assessment)

5. WELL Building Standard

Examples of Green Buildings Around the World:

a.   The Edge (Netherlands)

b.   Bosco Verticale (Italy)

c.   One Central Park (Australia)

d.   CII-Sohrabji Godrej Green Business Centre (India)

India's first platinum rated green building, emphasizing energy and water conservation.

Challenges in Green Building Implementation:

High Initial Costs: Green technology and materials may be costly.

Lack of Awareness: Developers and buyers may not prioritize sustainability.

Limited Skilled Workforce: Need for specialized training in green building techniques.

Policy & Regulatory Barriers: Insufficient government policies to enforce green standards.

5.1.1 Objectives of Green Buildings

1. Energy Efficiency

Reduce overall energy consumption through efficient design and technology.

Utilize renewable energy sources such as solar, wind and geothermal energy.

Incorporate energy efficient systems like LED lighting, smart HVAC systems and insulation.

2. Water Conservation

Minimize water wastage by using low flow fixtures and water efficient appliances.

Implement rainwater harvesting for irrigation and non-potable uses.

Promote greywater recycling for secondary use in toilets and landscaping.

3. Sustainable Material Use

Use eco-friendly, locally sourced and recyclable materials.

Reduce construction waste by adopting modular and prefabricated building techniques.

4. Indoor Environmental Quality (IEQ) Enhancement

Improve indoor air quality through proper ventilation and air filtration.

Maximize natural lighting and reduce artificial light dependency.

Ensure thermal comfort through adaptive insulation and efficient climate control.

5. Waste Management & Recycling

Reduce construction waste by implementing recycling process with composting systems.

Encourage on-site waste segregation to promote circular economy practices.

6. Climate Change Resilience

Design buildings to withstand extreme weather conditions (Floods, Earthquakes, Heatwaves).

Use passive cooling and heating techniques to adapt to climate variations.

Integrate green roofs and urban forests to reduce the urban heat island effect.

7. Reduction of Carbon Footprint

Lower greenhouse gas emissions by using clean energy and sustainable transport solutions.

Encourage low carbon construction materials and eco-friendly manufacturing.

Reduce reliance on fossil fuels through energy-efficient building operations.

8. Smart & Technology Integrated Buildings

Utilize automated lighting systems.

Adopt smart waste management systems for better resource utilization.

9. Enhancing Health & Well-Being

Reduce exposure to toxins by using natural, chemical-free materials.

Improve sound insulation to minimize noise pollution.

10. Cost-Effectiveness & Economic Benefits

Lower utility bills through energy and water efficiency.

Increase building lifespan through durable and low-maintenance materials.

Provide higher return on investment for green-certified properties.

5.1.2 uses

Uses of Green Buildings:

1. Energy Conservation & Efficiency

Reduce electricity consumption through energy efficient designs.

Utilize renewable energy sources (solar, wind, geothermal).

Lower carbon footprint and greenhouse gas emissions.

2. Water Conservation & Management

Minimize water wastage through low flow fixtures and rainwater harvesting.

Promote greywater recycling for landscaping and sanitation.

Reduce dependency on municipal water supplies.

3. Healthier Indoor Environment

Improve indoor air quality with proper ventilation and non-toxic materials.

Increase natural light and thermal comfort.

Reduce exposure to harmful chemicals and allergens.

4. Reduction in Operational Costs

Lower energy and water bills through efficient systems.

Reduce maintenance costs with durable and sustainable materials.

Increase property value and return on investment.

5. Sustainable Urban Development

Support eco-friendly city planning with green infrastructure.

Reduce urban heat island effect with green roofs and trees.

Improve waste management and recycling in cities.

6. Climate Change Mitigation

Reduce greenhouse gas emissions by using low carbon materials.

Design buildings to withstand extreme weather events.

7. Smart & Automated Buildings

Integrate AI automated lighting, heating and cooling.

Use real time monitoring for efficient energy and water use.

Enhance security and safety with smart building systems.

8. Green Commercial & Industrial Buildings

Improve workplace productivity and employee well-being.

Reduce operational costs for businesses.

9. Eco-Friendly Residential Developments

Lower utility bills for homeowners through energy efficient appliances.

Improve comfort and air quality with natural ventilation and insulation.

Reduce waste and promote sustainable living.

10. Educational & Institutional Green Buildings

Enhance learning environments with better air and light quality.

Reduce energy and water costs for schools and universities.

Promote environmental awareness and sustainability education.

5.1.3 Materials

Materials for Green Buildings:

Green building materials are eco-friendly, sustainable, energy efficient and durable, reducing the environmental impact of construction. These materials help conserve resources, improve indoor air quality and enhance building performance.

1. Sustainable & Recycled Materials such as Recycled Steel, Bamboo, Reclaimed Wood, Recycled Plastic etc.

2. Energy-Efficient Materials such as Hemp Crete (Hemp + Lime), Straw Bale, Aerated Autoclaved Concrete (AAC) etc.

3. Eco-Friendly Insulation Materials such as Sheep Wool Insulation, Cork Insulation, Cellulose Insulation etc.

4. Water Efficient & Permeable Materials such as Permeable Concrete, Pavers, Low-Flow Plumbing Fixtures etc.

5. Smart & Renewable Energy Materials such as Solar Glass, Photovoltaic Panels, Cool Roofing Materials etc.

6. Low Carbon & Non Toxic Finishing Materials such as Low-VOC Paints, Adhesives, Terrazzo Flooring etc.

7. Living & Biodegradable Materials such as Green Walls, Vertical Gardens, Mycelium (Mushroom based bricks) etc.

5.2 Certification Methods

Green Building Certification Methods:

Green building certification methods are standards that assess, verify and certify the sustainability, energy efficiency and environmental impact of buildings. These certifications help promote eco-friendly construction, improve building performance and encourage sustainable practices worldwide.

5.2.1 LEED, TERI, GRIHA, IGBC Certification

LEED (Leadership in Energy and Environmental Design):

This certification is followed by USA & Global, as well as administered by U.S. Green Building Council (USGBC). Used in over 180 countries for different building types such as Residential, commercial, institutional, industrial etc.

Certification Levels:

Sl. No.	Points	Grade
1	40 – 49	Certified
2	50 – 59	Silver
3	60 – 79	Gold
4	80+	Platinum

Evaluation Criteria is based on Energy efficiency (renewable energy, smart lighting, insulation), Water conservation (low-flow fixtures, rainwater harvesting), Material selection (recycled, locally sourced, non-toxic), Indoor environmental quality (natural ventilation, air filtration), Sustainable site selection & development.

LEED Certified Buildings in India are Infosys Campus, Bangalore (LEED Platinum) and ITC Green Centre, Gurgaon (LEED Platinum).

TERI (The Energy and Resources Institute):

This certification is Established by Government of India in 1974. Primary focus is on research and policy in sustainability, energy efficiency and environmental conservation. Functions:

Provides consultation for green buildings.

Works on climate change adaptation and mitigation.

Conducts sustainability research and training programs.

Supports the GRIHA green building rating system.

GRIHA (Green Rating for Integrated Habitat Assessment):

This certification is followed by The Energy and Resources Institute (TERI), as well as administered by India. Used in India for different Building Types such as Residential, commercial, industrial etc.

Certification Levels:

Sl. No.	Stars	Grade
1	25 - 40	1 Star
2	41 - 55	2 Star
3	56 - 70	3 Star
4	71 - 85	4 Star
5	86 +	5 Star

Evaluation Criteria is based on Site selection, Planning, Energy efficiency, water efficiency, Waste management, Materials, resources, Innovation & performance.

IGBC (Indian Green Building Council):

This certification is administered by Confederation of Indian Industry (CII) and it is applicable in India for the building such as Residential, Commercial, Hospitals, Hotels, Townships, Metro & Railway Stations.

IGBC Certification Levels:

Sl. No.	Points	Grade
1	40 – 49	Certified
2	50 – 59	Silver
3	60 – 74	Gold
4	75+	Platinum

IGBC Rating Categories & Evaluation Criteria:

Sustainable Site Planning: Eco-friendly land use, non-motorized transport and pedestrian-friendly designs.

Water Efficiency: Rainwater harvesting, water-efficient landscaping and reuse of treated water. Energy Efficiency: Renewable energy, high-performance HVAC and LED lighting.

Material Conservation: Use of low-carbon, recycled and sustainable materials.

Indoor Environmental Quality: Improved ventilation, use of non-toxic paints and daylight access.

Innovation & Design: Smart building automation and AI-powered sustainability solutions.

IGBC Certified Buildings in India are CII-Sohrabji Godrej Green Business Centre, Hyderabad (IGBC Platinum Certified) and TCS Tech Park, Chennai (IGBC Gold Certified).

Comparison of Green Building Certification Methods:

Sl. No.	Type of Certification	Region	Evaluation Criteria	Type of Building Applicable
1	LEED	Global	Energy, water, materials, site sustainability.	All buildings
2	TERI	India	energy efficiency and environmental conservation	Residential, commercial, industrial

3	GRIHA	India	Energy & water conservation.	Residential, commercial, industrial
4	IGBC	India	Eco friendly land use, Transport and Pedestrian friendly designs.	Residential, Commercial, Metro, Railway Stations.
5	BREEAM	UK, Europe	Climate resilience, Sustainability.	New & existing buildings
6	WELL	Global	Human health & well-being.	Offices, schools, healthcare
7	EDGE	Global	Cost-effective sustainability.	Affordable housing & commercial
8	NABERS	Australia	Energy & water efficiency.	Commercial buildings
9	DGNB	Germany, Europe	Life cycle sustainability.	Industrial & commercial

CHAPTER – VI

COMPUTER AIDED DRAWING (CAD)

Computer-Aided Drawing (CAD) is the use of computer software to create precise technical drawings and designs for architecture, engineering, manufacturing and other fields. CAD replaces traditional manual drafting with digital tools, improving accuracy, efficiency and flexibility in design. CAD is a fundamental tool for civil engineers because it is required for better planning, accurate designs and structural safety. It is used for designing buildings, highways or drainage systems. CAD is a revolutionary tool in design, engineering and construction. It enhances productivity, accuracy and collaboration, making it an essential skill for professionals in architecture, engineering and manufacturing.

6.1 Details and learning methods

Importance of CAD in Design & Engineering:

Precision & Accuracy: CAD allows for detailed measurements by reducing human errors. Efficiency: Saves time compared to manual drafting. Flexibility: Easy to edit, modify and duplicate designs. 3D Visualization: Helps in understanding spatial relationships.

Automation: Repetitive tasks can be automated (Dimensioning, Layering). Integration: CAD files can be used in 3D printing.

Types of CAD Software

2D CAD: Basic line drawings, floor plans, schematics.
3D CAD: Solid modeling, rendering and visualization.

Applications of CAD

Architecture use this software to draw Building plans, elevations, sections and 3D modeling. Mechanical Engineer use this software to draw Machine parts, gears and assemblies. This software is used in Automobile for the design of Car models.

Manufacturing industry use this software for Tool design and CNC programming. This software is used in Civil Engineering for the design of Road layouts, bridges and infrastructure.

6.2 Various Commands in CAD

CAD (Computer-Aided Design) software like AutoCAD, is used for creating 2D drawings and 3D models in engineering. To work efficiently in CAD, commands are used. These are short text inputs or clickable tools that allow users to quickly perform drawing, editing and modeling operations. In CAD software, a command is an instruction given to the program to perform a specific task. These commands can be typed into the Command Line (at the bottom of the screen in AutoCAD), selected from menus or triggered using keyboard shortcuts.

List of various commonly used 2D Commands in CAD software:

Sl. No.	Commands	Description
1	**LINE**	Draw a straight line.
2	**PLINE**	Draw a polyline (continuous line segment).
3	**CIRCLE**	Draw a circle.
4	**ARC**	Draw an arc.
5	**RECTANGLE**	Draw a rectangle.

6	**POLYGON**	Draw a polygon with a specified number of sides.
7	**ELLIPSE**	Draw an ellipse.
8	**MOVE**	Move objects from one place to another.
9	**COPY**	Copy objects to another location.
10	**ROTATE**	Rotate objects around a base point.
11	**SCALE**	Change the size of objects.
12	**TRIM**	Trim unwanted parts of lines, polylines, etc.
13	**EXTEND**	Extend objects to meet boundary edges.
14	**MIRROR**	Create a mirrored copy of selected objects.
15	**FILLET**	Round the edges where two lines meet.
16	**CHAMFER**	Create a beveled corner between two lines.
17	**OFFSET**	Create parallel copies of objects at a specified distance.
18	**STRETCH**	Stretch objects.
19	**TEXT**	Add single line text.
20	**MTEXT**	Add multi line text.
21	**DIM**	Create dimensions.
22	**LEADER**	Add a leader line with annotation.
23	**TABLE**	Create a table.
24	**LAYER**	Manage layers (create, delete, change properties).
25	**LAYERSTATE**	Save and restore layer states.
26	**LAYISO**	Isolate a layer (hide others).
27	**LAYUNISO**	Unisolate layers.
28	**ZOOM**	Zoom in/out.
29	**PAN**	Move the view horizontally/vertically.
30	**REGEN**	Regenerate the drawing to refresh display.
31	**VPORTS**	Set up multiple viewports.

32	**OSNAP**	Object snap settings.
33	**GRID**	Display a grid in the background.
34	**ORTHO**	Force horizontal/vertical lines.
35	**DIST**	Measure distance between two points.
36	**AREA**	Calculate area of a shape.
37	**LIST**	Display object properties.
38	**BLOCK**	Create a block.
39	**INSERT**	Insert a block.

List of various commonly used 2D Commands in CAD software:

Sl. No.	Commands	Description
40	**XREF**	Attach external references.
41	**EXPLODE**	Break objects into simpler components.
42	**NEW**	Start a new drawing.
43	**OPEN**	Open an existing drawing.
44	**SAVE**	Save the drawing.
45	**EXPORT**	Export to another file format (PDF, DWG etc.).
46	**UNDO**	Undo last action.
47	**REDO**	Redo last undone action.
48	**PROPERTIES**	Show object properties window.
49	**MATCHPROP**	Copy properties from one object to another.
50	**PURGE**	Remove unused elements (layers, blocks etc.).
51	**AUDIT**	Check drawing for errors.
52	**RECOVER**	Recover damaged files.

List of various commonly used 3D Commands in CAD software:

Sl. No.	Commands	Description
1	**BOX**	Creates a 3D solid box.
2	**SPHERE**	Creates a 3D solid sphere.
3	**CYLINDER**	Creates a 3D solid cylinder.
4	**CONE**	Creates a 3D solid cone.
5	**TORUS**	Creates a 3D solid torus (donut shape).
6	**WEDGE**	Creates a 3D wedge shape.
7	**EXTRUDE**	Extrudes a 2D shape into a 3D solid.
8	**PRESSPULL**	Press or pull closed areas to create/extrude solids.
9	**REVOLVE**	Revolves a 2D shape around an axis to create a 3D object.
10	**POLYSOLID**	Creates a 3D wall-like solid from lines/polylines.
11	**UNION**	Combines two or more solids into one.
12	**SUBTRACT**	Subtracts one solid from another.
13	**INTERSECT**	Creates a solid from overlapping portions of solids.
14	**SLICE**	Cuts a solid into two along a plane.
15	**FILLETEDGE**	Adds a fillet to the edges of a solid.
16	**CHAMFEREDGE**	Adds a chamfer to the edges of a solid.
17	**SHELL**	Removes faces from a solid and creates a hollow object.
18	**MOVE**	Moves objects in 3D space.
19	**ROTATE3D**	Rotates objects around a 3D axis.
20	**ALIGN**	Aligns objects in 3D space.
21	**MIRROR3D**	Creates a mirrored copy of a 3D object.

List of various commonly used 3D Commands in CAD software:

Sl. No.	Commands	Description

22	**SCALE**	Scales a 3D object.
23	**SURFNETWORK**	Creates a surface through a network of curves.
24	**SURFOFFSET**	Creates a parallel surface at a specified offset distance.
25	**SURFPATCH**	Creates a surface patch between edges.
26	**SURFEXTRACT**	Extracts isoline curves from a surface.
27	**MESH**	Creates 3D meshes like boxes, spheres, or cones.
28	**MESHSMOOTH**	Smoothens mesh objects.
29	**MESHREFINE**	Refines the mesh into smaller faces.
30	**CONVERTMESH**	Converts mesh to solid or surface.
31	**3DORBIT**	Rotates the view around objects interactively.
32	**VPOINT**	Sets 3D viewpoint using X, Y, Z coordinates.
33	**VIEW**	Saves and manages custom views.
34	**NAVSWHEEL**	Opens a 3D navigation wheel (pan, zoom, orbit etc.).
35	**UCS**	Manages the User Coordinate System in 3D space.
36	**PLAN**	Sets the view perpendicular to the current UCS.
37	**MATERIALS**	Opens materials browser.
38	**RENDER**	Generates a rendered image of the 3D model.
39	**LIGHT**	Adds or manages lights in the model.
40	**CAMERA**	Places a camera for perspective views.
41	**SECTIONPLANE**	Creates a section plane through 3D objects.
42	**XEDGES**	Extracts edges from solids or surfaces into 2D geometry.
43	**CONVTOSOLID**	Converts surfaces to solids (if closed).
44	**CONVTOSURFACE**	Converts solids to surfaces.
45	**FLATSHOT**	Creates a 2D projection of 3D objects.

About the Authors & Editors

Prof. Santosh Mahadev Kinayekar (MTech in Structural Engineering), is presently working as Assistant Professor and Head of Research and Development cell in Civil Engineering Department at Alamuri Ratnamala Institute of Engineering & Technology, Shahapur, Thane Mumbai University. He completed his Engineering and Master's degree from Visvesvaraya Technological University, Belgaum, Karnataka, currently pursuing Ph.D. in Civil Engineering. He published more than 21 Research papers in various International Journals and presented paper in National and International Conference. He published 01 Utility Patent and 08 Indian Design Patents and Granted 3 Patents. He has more than 12 years of experience in Teaching and Administration. He is an Associate Member of the IRED (Institute of Research Engineers and Doctors). He taken Guest lecture on Advance Surveying and AutoCAD 2D Drafting. Authors have his own YouTube channel, "Prof. santosh kinayekar Civil Engineer" on YouTube https://www.youtube.com/channel/UCkc7lZB5FvUN6YfY29rwiow

Dr. Prashant Ramesh Bamane (Ph.D. in Civil Engineering), is presently working as Associate Professor and Head of Civil Engineering Department at G.V.Acharya Institute of Engineering and Technology, Shelu, Mumbai University. He completed his Master of Engineering and Bachelor of Engineering from Government College of Engineering, Karad. He published more than 20 Research papers in International and Nation journals. He published 1 utility and 3 Indian Design Patents. He has more than 10 years of Academic and Administration experience. Also he has taken various guest lectures and also Presented as a Session chair for International conferences. He received 2 awards for his contribution in academic field. He is member of various Professional Bodies I.e. IGS etc.

Dr. Shobhan Sadhan Kelkar (Ph.D. in Architecture) is working as Professor and Head of the Department at STES' Smt. Kashibai Navale College of Architecture, Pune. She completed his Bachelor of Architecture, Master of Architecture (M.Arch in Architectural and Construction Project Management) and Ph.D. in Architecture. She has a good academic experience of 24 years in the field of Architecture along with professional experience. She had been awarded for excellence in academics 2021, Architecture & Interior Design Excellence Awards at Bangalore and also Awarded 'Best Teacher' by Yashwant Vidyapeeth, Karad in 2015. She published research papers in various national and international journals, presented papers at national and international conferences. In addition to research, she has developed and delivered engaging lectures, designed course materials and mentored students. She is associated with various institutes and universities as a resource person, examiner and various committee member. She is a registered member of the Council of Architecture, the Indian Institute of Architects and one of the founder member of IIA- sub center Karad, Maharashtra, India.

Dr. Akshay Wayal (Ph.D. in Architecture), is presently working as an Assistant Professor at MIT ADT University, School of Architecture, Pune. He completed his Bachelor of Architecture (B.Arch) and Master of Architecture (M.Arch Construction Management) from Savitribai Phule Pune University, Pune, Maharashtra. He has Also Completed his Ph.D from Shri. Jagdishprasad Jhabharmal Tibrewala University (Shri. J.J.T University), Rajasthan, India. He has published research papers in various international journals and presented papers at national and international conferences. He is a registered Architect of the Council of Architecture (COA), New Delhi, India. His work in the field of Architecture Education has also been recognized in "Bombay Filmfame Magazine" where he has shared his perspectives on architecture and education.

Dr. Ajinkya Pradeep Niphadkar is an Associate Professor with over 11 years of experience in the field of Architecture. He holds a PhD and Master's degree in Sustainable Architecture and a Bachelor's degree in Architecture. His areas of expertise include water conservation, energy-efficient materials, vernacular architecture, passive cooling techniques, and climate-responsive building designs. He has authored numerous research papers, focusing on tropical climates, building technology and the integration of sustainable practices in residential and urban design. He has co-authored works on disaster management, affordable housing and parametric design and has contributed to several national and international conferences. His research also explores innovative teaching methods for architectural students, particularly for rural backgrounds and Marathi medium candidates. He is a registered member of the Council of Architecture, the Indian Institute of Architects, Indian Institute of Interior Designers and other architectural organizations. He has received the Best Research Paper Award at an international conference and is actively involved in various academic and professional committees.

Prof. Amruta Yogesh Raskar (M.E. in Geotechnical Engineering), is working as Assistant Professor at G H Raisoni College of Engineering and Management, Pune, currently pursuing PhD in Geotechnical Engineering. She has a good academic experience of 08 years, along with professional experience. She published Research papers in various International Journals and presented paper in National and International Conference.